Developing and Leading Emergence Teams

Developing and Leading Emergence Teams addresses a business landscape that is at times simple, complicated, complex or chaotic, and where the variety and diversity of the environments within which organizations operate require a corresponding variety of organizational practices if they are to respond successfully to emerging opportunities.

To successfully grasp these opportunities, Smith and Cockburn describe a unique approach based on what they term as *emergence teams*: high-trust teams that exhibit exceptional affinity for knowledge sharing, sense making, and consensus building that give them the ability to accurately define the business environment that the organization is facing and recommend appropriate action. The authors explore the specifics of forming and leading these unique teams, including how a team leader should interact and facilitate the team's development; understand the personal nature of each of the team members; and the overall emotional regime that will affect trust, commitment and motivation. The skills that emergence team members must possess or develop are also detailed. A case study is described that clarifies how an emergence team is formed and operates under typical organizational constraints.

Throughout the book, Smith and Cockburn draw on research and their own practical experience to provide techniques your organization can readily adopt to organize and support an emergence team approach. This will ensure your organization has the capability to respond successfully to emerging business opportunities.

Peter A.C. Smith is President and CEO of The Leadership Alliance Inc. (TLA), a global consortium of authorities in disciplines relevant to identifying and resolving VUCA. He is also Director, Center Strategy for the Center for Dynamic Leadership Models in Global Business.

Tom Cockburn's leadership and management experience includes five years' Board experience on the Standing Conference of Welsh Management Education Centres in the UK, building capability and enhancing quality provision across the tertiary sector in Wales and a year as board member on the Board of Trustees of K'aute Pasifika Trust in New Zealand.

Developing and Leading Emergence Teams

A new approach for identifying and resolving complex business problems

PETER A.C. SMITH
AND TOM COCKBURN
The Leadership Alliance Inc.

LONDON AND NEW YORK

First published 2016
by Routledge
2 Park Square, Milton Park, Abingdon, Oxon OX14 4RN

and by Routledge
711 Third Avenue, New York, NY 10017

Routledge is an imprint of the Taylor & Francis Group, an informa business

© 2016 Peter A.C. Smith and Tom Cockburn

The right of Peter A.C. Smith and Tom Cockburn to be identified as the authors of this work has been asserted by them in accordance with sections 77 and 78 of the Copyright, Designs and Patents Act 1988.

All rights reserved. No part of this book may be reprinted or reproduced or utilised in any form or by any electronic, mechanical, or other means, now known or hereafter invented, including photocopying and recording, or in any information storage or retrieval system, without permission in writing from the publishers.

Trademark notice: Product or corporate names may be trademarks or registered trademarks, and are used only for identification and explanation without intent to infringe.

British Library Cataloguing in Publication Data
A catalogue record for this book is available from the British Library

Library of Congress Cataloging-in-Publication Data
Names: Smith, Peter A. C., 1933– author. | Cockburn, Tom, 1949– author.
Title: Developing and leading emergence teams : a new approach for
   identifying and resolving complex business problems / by Peter A.C. Smith and
   Tom Cockburn.
Description: Burlington, VT : Gower, 2016. | Includes bibliographical
   references and index.
Identifiers: LCCN 2015034484 | ISBN 9781472460349 (hardback : alk. paper) |
   ISBN 9781472460356 (ebook) | ISBN 9781472460363 (epub)
Subjects: LCSH: Teams in the workplace. | Leadership. | Problem solving.
Classification: LCC HD66 .S635 2016 | DDC 658.4/022—dc23
LC record available at HYPERLINK "https://protect-us.mimecast.com/s/rx4mBRUdm713hW"
   http://lccn.loc.gov/2015034484

ISBN: 978-1-4724-6034-9 (hbk)
ISBN: 978-1-315-57680-0 (ebk)

Typeset in Sabon
by Apex CoVantage, LLC

Printed in the United Kingdom by Henry Ling Limited, at the Dorset Press, Dorchester, DT1 1HD

Contents

List of figures vii
Foreword ix
Preface xv

1	Introducing the emergence team approach	1
2	Team context definition and consensus building	17
3	Establishing an emergence team	33
4	Team leader insights	49
5	Emergence team dynamics	67
6	Team members' insights	85
7	Team intelligence-in-action	100
8	Digital technology and emerging teams	119
9	Future research impact	140
10	Revised case study	150

Acknowledgement 165
Index 167

Figures

1.1	Cynefin framework	3
4.1	Dynamic performance system	51
4.2	Leadership learning cycle	53
5.1	Spiral through metaphor to metonymy	71
6.1	Relationships between Cynefin contexts and performance drivers	92
7.1	Matrix of emotional regimes exhibited in teams	112
7.2	Representation of the 3D chart of team development	114

Foreword

We live in an era . . . we're all ballroom dancing in the minefield.
Andrew Zolli

Emergence teams – your guide to leading organizations in 'the fog of VUCA'.

What you have in your hands is a thoughtful, theoretically informed yet grounded guide for those who want their organization to 'have the last word' and not merely survive, but thrive in a global business environment that is a veritable minefield of Volatility, Uncertainty, Complexity and Ambiguity (VUCA).

Actually, even more so, this book is a superb guide to Antifragility. In fact, while Nassim Nicholas Taleb paints for us a picture of the new world of randomness, uncertainty and chaos in broad brush strokes, Peter and Tom present us with what I can best describe as a carefully detailed dot painting in the style of Australian Aboriginal art that enables organizations to deepen their understanding of, and capably respond to, the new realities of an uncertain and increasingly volatile global business world.

As I am writing this foreword, over half a million refugees from the Middle East are pouring into Europe, the Shanghai stock market is in an alarming slump, China's economic slow-down is deepening, a drought is hitting much of India's agricultural heartland state of Maharashtra, and the US–Iran deal is under threat with greater turmoil in the Middle East even more likely. It is clear that change, turbulent, disruptive and unpredictable change, is here, and is here to stay. Predictions are that it will more likely get worse.

Tellingly, Thomas Friedman in his book *The World is Flat* vividly confirms how change today is fast, pervasive and global in its scale and impact, and is therefore much different and more profound than ever in the past. Today's changes, he argues, are 'qualitatively different from other such great changes of previous eras: the speed and breadth with which it is taking hold . . . is happening at warp speed and directly or indirectly touching a lot more people on the planet at once. The faster and broader this transition to a new era, the greater the potential for disruption' (Friedman, 2007, p. 49).

This disruptive volatility is creating what business leaders and analysts increasing call a fragile 'VUCA' environment. Coined in the late 1990s, the military-derived acronym stands for volatility, uncertainty, complexity and ambiguity. However, VUCA is more than just some trendy managerial acronym. These features tell us that we have crossed over into a very different, unstable and fast-paced business environment in which the market is characterized by sheer volatility, prone to wicked higher and lower shifts, in which it is not unusual for the Dow Jones industrial average to travel thousands of points in either direction in some trading sessions.

At this juncture though, this book reminds us that we must keep two points in mind. First, that VUCA conflates four distinct types of challenges that demand four distinct types of responses. Challenging as these situations will be, you have here, in this book, an evidence-based emergence team strategy ideally placed to address these extreme demands. Second, yes, VUCA resembles a minefield, but any impression that it is an unmanageable chaotic field out there is also misleading. Yes, VUCA does make it very difficult to know how to approach these multiple challenging situations. VUCA does demand a holistic set of diverse strategies capable of covering multiple bases and possibilities simultaneously. But no, as Peter and Tom will show you, VUCA is not an excuse to despair and abandon the hard work of strategy and planning. They demonstrate how we can navigate this new and unpredictable world bravely, safely and successfully, using emergence teams.

I will leave it to them to explain the power of these teams in the following chapters, suffice to say that they are eminently equipped to help us navigate our way through what can best be described as 'the fog of VUCA' and more so to assist you and your organization to effectively modify your strategies and develop initiatives to operate confidently and successfully in a VUCA environment.

Both Peter and Tom are not just mere scholars but are organizational leadership practitioners par excellence. They not only possess a tremendous wealth of knowledge but, most importantly, their feet are always firmly planted in the real world of organizational leadership.

Peter has a long, distinguished record in providing strategic consulting, business planning and leadership development programmes. His list of blue ribbon clients includes KPMG, Bank of England, IKEA, Glaxo-Smith Kline, AT&T, Canada National Rail and the City of London. He is currently President of The Leadership Alliance Inc. (TLA), and maintains a worldwide consulting practice assisting leading public and private sector organizations optimize their leadership and organizational capabilities. Tom has an international consulting and leadership experience portfolio that includes international quality reviews of MBAs as well as consulting team leadership in the EU, Australia, New Zealand and the UK. This included being head of the third largest business school in Wales for over eight years before returning to the private consulting field in 2001. He works with Henley International Management College and with the Department of International Business at the University of Ulster, and is currently Director (policy) for the Center for Dynamic Leadership Models in Global Business and a senior associate of The Leadership Alliance Inc., headquartered in Canada.

Far from being a survival guide to the world of VUCA, their focus is clearly on one goal: *how to enable organizations to have the last word and thrive* because all this turbulence creates a fertile playing field for a new and novel approach to organizational teams. They clearly point to the power of these new 'emergence teams' to 'antifragile-proof' their organizations. What I particularly appreciate is that, while novel, the emergence team concept builds on a synthesis of the most solid, evidence-based experiences of what I, in my own work, call 'Participatory Action Learning'. What Nassim Nicholas Taleb has started, Peter Smith and Tom Cockburn finish with the able assistance of the valuable work of Reg Revans, the founder and eminent practitioner of action learning.

Emergence teams are specifically designed to respond effectively to randomness and uncertainty. To borrow from Nassim Nicholas Taleb, these antifragility emergence teams enable organizations to deal with the unknown, to do things without always fully understanding them – and do them well. As Bob Johansen notes, the positive flip side of VUCA is Vision, Understanding, Clarity and Agility, and this is precisely what emergence teams offer! By developing the concept of emergence teams, Peter and Tom have grasped the mechanisms of antifragility. They give us a practical guide to non-predictive decision making and practice in complex situations fraught with randomness, unpredictability and opacity. In a nutshell, emergence teams harness antifragility!

If predicting trends is not at all clear, what is patently clear is that this turbulent VUCA landscape calls for agile, responsive and, above all, antifragile organizations that deploy emergence teams in order to not just survive but thrive in a VUCA world.

What is also clear is that this book is *not* about being resilient in a fragile world, it is much more than that. This book takes you far beyond resilience. As Nassim Nicholas Taleb points out, 'the resilient resists shocks and stays the same; the antifragile gets better'. Emergence teams help your organization to be antifragile; not just to survive uncertainty, not just to 'make it', but as Taleb puts it, to keep getting better and above all, 'to have the last word!' and be robustly antifragile in the world of VUCA. Thus, participatory action learning-based emergence teams are the key to 'domesticate, dominate, even conquer, the unseen, the opaque, and the inexplicable' world of VUCA.

I know you will enjoy this book as Peter and Tom, as the most able of organizational dance-masters, show you how to dance with style and confidence through the VUCA minefield.

Henk Eijkman

Canberra
Management Board
Asia–Pacific Alliance for Quality Assurance in
Higher Education (APAQA-HE)

References

Bennet, N. and Lemoine, G.J. 2014. What VUCA really means for you. *Harvard Business Review*, Jan–Feb, Available at: https://hbr.org/2014/01/what-vuca-really-means-for-you [Accessed 14 September 2015].

Cox, J. 2015 Volatile market crosses into a 'different world' CNBC, 1 September 2015. Available at: <http://www.cnbc.com/2015/09/01/volatile-market-crosses-into-a-different-world.html> [Accessed 14 September 2015].

Friedman, T. L. 2007. *The World is Flat 3.0: A Brief History of the 21st Century*. New York: Picador.

Githens, G. 2015. Volatility, Uncertainty, Complexity, & Ambiguity (VUCA). Available at: <http://leadingstrategicinitiatives.com/2015/02/27/volatility-uncertainty-complexity-ambiguity-vuca/> [Accessed 14 September 2015].

Gratton, L. 2015. Building resilience in a fragile world, *Harvard Business Review*. Available at: <https://hbr.org/product/building-resilience-in-a-fragile-world/ROT258-PDF-ENG> [Accessed 14 September 2015].

Gulati, R. 2010. Reorganize for resilience: Putting customers at the center of your business, *Harvard Business Review*. Available at: <https://hbr.org/product/reorganize-for-resilience-putting-customers-at-the-center-of-your-business/1721E-KND-ENG> [Accessed 14 September 2015].

Lawrence, K. 2013 Developing leaders in a VUCA environment. UNC Kenan-Flagler Business School. Available at: <http://www.kenan-flagler.unc.edu/executive-development/about/~/media/Files/documents/executive-development/developing-leaders-in-a-vuca-environment.pdf> [Accessed 14 September 2015].

Taleb, N. N. 2012. *Antifragile: Things that Gain from Disorder*. London: Penguin Books.

Zolli, A. and Green, S. 2012. Resilience strategies for a fragile world, *Harvard Business Review*. Available at: <https://hbr.org/2012/07/resilience-strategies-for-a-vo> [Accessed 14 September 2015].

Preface

We premise this book on our belief that the global business environment has changed dramatically and that 'Normal' based on applying 'Best Practice' is a thing of the past. In our two previous books (Smith and Cockburn, 2013; 2014) we detailed the extensive evidence on which this belief is based, plus our recommendations for new leadership capability development to address this environment. The reality is that everyone is now challenged to live and work in the world of VUCA – an acronym used to stand for today's volatile, uncertain, often complex, and ambiguous business conditions and situations. We do not contend that all past experience must be ignored but rather that the tacit components of organizational knowledge must be made explicit and then carefully evaluated to guide organizational planning and action based on experimentation. We fully agree with McKinsey & Company (2014) who asserts that this new environment is 'rich in possibilities for those who are prepared' – we authored this new book that describes the purpose, development, and activities of emergence teams, to insure that its readers are indeed well prepared to take full advantage of workplace possibilities.

Emergence team initiatives are specifically designed to assist organizations to successfully do business in our VUCA world by exploring and questioning the organizational tacit knowledge they possess and formulating further action based on continuous learning and action based on the experimental approach of 'probe, sense and respond'.

We have written this book in particular for senior organizational executives and the emergence team sponsor(s), plus interested experienced practitioners, to provide them with a detailed practical introduction to emergence teams. Our book includes important relevant background information and case studies, and it is structured to provide a step-wise narrative setting out detailed guidance regarding ongoing emergence team activities. It will be invaluable in assisting the emergence team leader provide leadership for the emergence team, and also, very importantly, it provides practical knowledge and guidance with regard to emergence team activities for the emergence team members themselves.

Peter A.C. Smith and Dr Tom Cockburn

References

McKinsey & Company, 2014. Insights and publications, the new normal. Available at: <http://www.mckinsey.com/insights/strategy/the_new_normal> [Retrieved 11 July 2014].

Smith, P.A.C. and Cockburn, T., 2013. *Dynamic Leadership Models for Global Business: Enhancing Digitally Connected Environments*. Hershey, PA: IGI Global.

Smith, P.A.C. and Cockburn, T., eds., 2014. *Impact of Emerging Digital Technologies on Leadership in Global Business*. Hershey, PA: IGI Global.

Chapter 1
Introducing the emergence team approach

The global business landscape has changed fundamentally and 'normal' is a thing of the past. This is the assertion made by Deloitte (2014) based on their research on global business indices. They affirm that everyone is now working in the world of VUCA – an acronym used to stand for the volatility, uncertainty, complexity and ambiguity of general business conditions and situations. However, according to McKinsey & Company (2014) this new environment is 'rich in possibilities for those who are prepared'. Our book ensures that its readers are indeed well prepared.

More specifically, our book is intended for senior executives and the emergence team sponsor(s) plus interested experienced practitioners, to provide them with an introduction to emergence teams including relevant significant background information, and specific guidance for ongoing emergence team activities. Secondly it is intended to assist the team leader in providing leadership for the emergence team and specific guidance in ongoing emergence team activities. Lastly, but very importantly, it provides practical knowledge and guidance with regard to team activities for the emergence team members.

Chapters 1 through 10 in this book are structured to provide a step-wise flow setting out:

- A general overview of the emergence team approach to significant, often complex, organizational problems; and describing a 'base' case study.

- The process of reaching consensus on the issues encountered by the team, including how to reach agreement on the context of the emergence team intervention plus a description of the sponsor's role in the intervention.

- In what fashion the emergence team should be formed plus how the team leader, team members and interviewees should be chosen.

- Knowledge regarding the intervention that is vital for the team leader to possess and understand.

- Emergence team dynamics including theoretical fundamentals.

- Details of the skills and techniques that emergence team members must master.

- Details on embodying and embedding team intelligence-in-action.

- Digital technology options to facilitate emergence teamwork.

- The impact of future research on emergence teams.

- A revised case study of the case that was first sketched out in Chapter 1; this chapter indicates how that case would have been addressed using an emergence team approach.

Chapter 1 provides a foundation for appreciating why emergence teams hold the key to high performance in VUCA environments, and a framework for recognizing the value of later chapters. This book is a compilation of practical insights for readers to reflect upon and apply as appropriate; these insights are drawn from the authors' extensive research and experience.

The Cynefin framework

Organizations typically try to apply simplified solutions to even the most urgent problems because they lack 'situational awareness'. All too often they are trying to solve the wrong problem as they confuse symptoms and causes. This failure to attain expected results in spite of great effort is to a great extent attributable to the emergence of a new, unique class of problems for which conventional approaches and solutions are inadequate.

The nature of the issues facing leaders and practitioners as they grapple with the variety of problems they face is exemplified in Figure 1.1. This framework was developed by Dave Snowden (Snowden, 2014) to help define the kinds of actions that practitioners may gainfully apply in different business environments. It assists in determining the degree of business complexity in which practitioners are operating and the appropriate steps to take. As Figure 1.1 shows, each

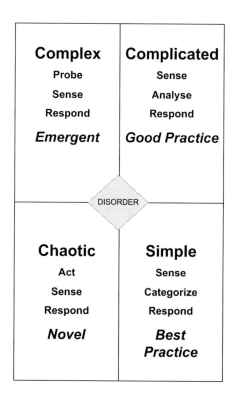

Figure 1.1 Cynefin framework
Source: Adapted from Snowden, 2014

environment requires different actions. Snowden and Boone (2007) detail application of the framework and explain how informed decision makers tailor their approach to fit the environment they face.

It should be no surprise to decision makers when previously successful problem solving approaches fail in new situations. Organizations typically try to apply simplified solutions to even the most urgent problems because they lack 'situational awareness'. All too often they are trying to solve the wrong problem as they confuse symptoms and causes. The simple reason is that most organizations try to solve problems facing backwards! They confidently assert that what worked in the past will work in the future – try driving your car down a busy street that way. You'll end up in the same 'pickle' as do such organizations – with a catastrophe! As Snowden and Boone (2007) assert: different contexts call for different kinds of responses. Before addressing a situation, leaders need to recognize which context governs it and tailor afresh their actions. To facilitate this, Snowden and Boone have formed a new perspective on decision making – the Cynefin framework – which they have based on complexity science. This framework assists leaders sort issues into five contexts as shown in Figure 1.1. The Cynefin framework may be interpreted and applied as described in the following paragraphs.

As Figure 1.1 indicates, simple contexts are characterized by stable cause-and-effect relationships that will be quickly evident to the majority of practitioners. In these stable contexts, decision makers must first 'sense' and affirm this context, then respond to it appropriately. Complicated contexts may contain multiple right answers, and though there is a clear relationship between cause and effect, not everyone can see it. Here, leaders must sense, analyse and respond. Senge (1990, p. 71) called this context 'detailed complexity' and likened it to mixing many ingredients in a stew or to a lengthy set of instructions for assembling a machine. The complex context is the realm of VUCA where correct answers cannot be inferred, and indeed, simply "searching for right answers is pointless" according to Snowden and Boone (2007, p. 5) since the results of a single intervention will not be obvious. However these authors claim that by first probing, then sensing, and then responding appropriately (doing no harm), instructive patterns will eventually emerge leading to problem resolution. In the complex context, caution must be exercised in regard to 'quick fixes' since problems may seem to be solved in the short term although even more serious problems may have been caused that may occur in the long term. Five approaches for managing in a complex context have been described by Snowden and Boone (2007, p. 6):

1. 'Open up the discussion, more interaction is required than in any other context

2. Set barriers to delineate behavior

3. Stimulate attractors – probes that resonate with people

4. Encourage dissent and diversity

5. Focus on creating an environment within which good things may emerge rather than trying to bring about predetermined results'

The chaotic realm is one of disorder, and exhibits dynamic shifting relationships between cause and effect that are impossible to determine, because they shift constantly and no manageable patterns exist. In this domain, the decision maker must first act to establish order, then sense where stability is present, and finally work to transform the situation from chaos to complexity.

The fifth context is disorder, and applies when it is unclear which of the other four contexts is predominant. The way out involves breaking the situation into its constituent parts and assigning each to one of the other four realms. Leaders can then make decisions and intervene in contextually appropriate ways. Extreme caution must be exercised in this context, since as Russell Ackoff (1977) warned 50 years ago, problems occur in systems which Ackoff termed 'messes'; every time we try to solve one problem in isolation we simply create new problems that add to the mess.

Snowden and Boone (2007) describe the Cynefin framework as a tool for a leader to use in their decision making. Snowden (2010) describes the Cynefin framework as a 'sense-making framework which is socially constructed from peoples' experience of their past and also their anticipated futures . . . and is normally created as an emergent property of social interaction. One of the reasons for this is the need to root any sense-making model in peoples' own understanding of their past and possible futures'. With this in mind, in our view, the use of the framework solely by leaders seriously short-changes its power, and in this book we recommend its use in team settings where conclusions drawn regarding environments and responses are emergent, enriched and reached by consensus based on organizational knowledge, team consensus or team input to the leader.

Cynefin is a Welsh word, which may be translated into English as 'place', although the term was chosen by Snowden (2014) to describe his understanding of the evolutionary nature of complex systems, and their inherent uncertainty – the name Cynefin is his reminder that all human interactions are emergent and determined by experiences, both through the direct influence of personal experience, and through collective experience; for example through storytelling.

The four Cynefin environments and associated recommended responses are:

1   Simple environment: sense–categorize–respond.

2   Complicated environment: sense–analyse–respond.

3   Complex environment: probe–sense–respond.

4   Chaotic environment: act–sense–respond.

Many organizations categorize the environments they face without any examination as 'known environments', assuming, without further study, that the environments in question have been previously categorized. These organizations then respond by applying 'best practices'; that is solutions that have worked in the past. However in our VUCA business world, where complex conditions exist in virtually all business situations, 'Normal' no longer applies and employing 'best practices' without very careful consideration does not take account of surprise factors and indeed often produces catastrophic results. In this regard, it is noteworthy that the average longevity of S&P 500 organizations declined from 67 years in the 1920s to just 15 years today (Gittleson, 2014).

Application of Cynefin response #2 may seem to offer a safer, more general situational approach although 'analysis' too has many pitfalls (Ackoff, 1981) and this environment would be better approached using systems theory (Ackoff, 1981). For example, analysis would not resolve the following question: why do two seemingly identical cars have the steering wheel on the left in one case and on the right in the other? A systems approach could tell us that one is built for the UK market and the other for the North American market.

Action learning

The experimental approach of 'probe, sense and respond' may seem to many practitioners unusual and overly cautious and demanding, although it is one that has served countless organizations well for many decades, for example, in complex plant optimization using statistical design and analysis, and also in organizational development where it is called 'action learning' (Revans, 1996). We recommend that the process of action learning be undertaken by an emergence team in sensemaking within the Cynefin framework as they explore the information generated from the interviews team members hold with organizational members. Some descriptive details of the action learning process are provided later in this chapter, and further practical details are provided in later chapters.

It is very important that the organization's management and members of the emergence team understand the significance of learning for successful application of the Cynefin framework. Upon the detection of an error, most people look for 'a quick fix', that is another operational strategy that will work within the same goal-structure and rule-boundaries. This is 'single-loop learning' (Argyris, 1991) involving a simple feedback loop, where outcomes cause adjustment of behaviours, like a thermostat. This is generally the case when goals, beliefs, values, conceptual frameworks and strategies are taken for granted without critical reflection. A higher order of learning is realized when the emergence team, upon detecting a mismatch between the target organizational performance and reality, questions the goal-structures and rules that resulted in the performance realized; this is double-loop learning. It is critical to make sure that the emergence team's action learning activity result in a 'probe' that will not produce disastrous results but rather provides the double-loop learning from which careful further probing may be planned after in-depth reflection via action learning (sensing, adapting). Although slow, this approach has no serious drawbacks, even when Cynefin environments #1 or #2 are actually being faced.

Action learning typically takes place among trusted colleagues in a group of about six people where the group ('Set') members encourage and help the group member(s) owning the problem to reflect on problem causes and possible courses of action before the Set member(s) with responsibility for the problem take(s) action. The action learning approach practised in organizations today has become highly structured and consultant/Set adviser-driven. For the generic purposes of this book we recommend the original approach pioneered by the founder of action learning in the 1940s – Professor Reg Revans (1996), or the well-respected variant introduced by Roger Gaunt (1991) which recognizes 'emotion' as a significant initiator of problems. Revans established action learning in very approachable terms in the 1940s, for example with groups of coal miners in the UK, based on the notion of an ad hoc group of colleagues sharing and reflecting on their practical experience and developing questions through which they might further learn and take reasoned action. The action learning cycle of taking action, reflecting on results and taking further action is repeated as necessary, forming the basis of an interactive step-wise adaptive (emergent) process comparable to the Cynefin process steps.

Smith (1997a) explains that, epistemologically, learning has typically been equated with the detection and correction of error and psychologists have traditionally associated learning with an invariant context (Weick, 1991). Since as explained above, rapid and large-scale contextual change may be considered the norm in today's business, an invariant context does not exist, and trying to learn about the business environment by applying action learning may seem quite inappropriate. In contrast, the term *adaption* has typically been used by social scientists in situations where the context changes and the organization accordingly adapts itself or its environment (Ackoff and Emery, 1972). Revans (1982, 1984a) himself seems to have foreseen this confusion but chose simply to interpret 'adapting' as 'learning' since as he himself said, 'Our ability to adapt to change with such readiness that we are seen to benefit may be defined as "learning"'. In this way he justified his using the term action learning, and we justify its use by emergence teams as described in this book.

It is clear that the Cynefin framework is intended as a means to ultimately take effective action, and in this regard Revans emphasized from the beginning that this was one of his principal intentions for action learning. For example, he wrote the following as a definition of action learning: 'We are trying to encourage managers to discover how they can pose fresh questions in conditions of ignorance, risk and confusion; first to design a new course of action; second to implement the course of action' (Revans, 1984a). Revans (1982) also stated that action learning operates only under conditions where a general theory of search is infeasible and where learning must be picked up 'minute by minute, as the changes and their risks come out of the blue' (Revans, 1983). In another article, Revans (1984b) provided an even more graphic description of the exaggerated turbulence and change he believed loomed before people and organizations in the twentieth century. In this article he likens this change to an ever-steeper precipice on which we are forced to climb and live. What we need to know according to Revans is: 'How do I ask myself questions about the future? . . . How do I guess the things *most likely* to happen? Nothing, of course, is absolutely predictable. All the same, it would be reassuring to define what is most probable.' Clearly action learning is relevant for an emergence team to adopt as the team explores an organization's situation within the Cynefin framework.

Based on extensive experience with significant strategic change projects in a variety of organizations (Smith, 1993; Smith and Saint-Onge, 1996), Smith (1997b) proposed a practical dynamic systemic questioning variant of action learning which is consistent with the tenets of action learning and which broadens the choices for problem – structuring/problem solving – and which addresses 'learning to do things right', 'learning to do the right things' and 'learning to learn'. Smith (1997b) demonstrated that this form of action learning remains consistent with the aims of Revan's (1971) action learning governing Systems Beta, Alpha and Gamma, and with Revans's intention to set up conditions in which 'Comrades in adversity learn from and with each other through discriminating questioning, fresh experience and reflective insight'. Smith's form of action learning is recommended for use by emergence teams and details of its application will be provided in Chapter 6; references to action learning in other chapters are consistent with Smith's action learning variant.

The Virtual Action Learning work of Waddil (2004; 2006) demonstrates that action learning may also be carried out very successfully online; this approach is particularly relevant to emergence teams when team members are widely dispersed. Much of the learning wisdom embodied in action learning may be used in the context of 'probe, sense and respond' espoused in the Cynefin approach, and the application of action learning in this online context are described in later chapters.

Emergence and emergence teams

Application of the Cynefin framework raises a number of practical questions: What is the best way to categorize the environment facing an organization? Once categorized, what is the best way to decide on a response or a series of responses? This book answers these questions and is all about 'emergence teams'. Let us explore here what we mean by 'emergence' and, given the wide variety of teams operating in organizations, why this one is called an 'emergence team'.

According to Wikipedia (2015) emergence is a process whereby a system, entity, pattern or regularity with singular properties evolves through interactions among smaller, simpler entities, that themselves do not exhibit such properties The characteristics of emergence are: (1) radical novelty (features not previously observed in systems); (2) coherence or correlation (integrated wholes that maintain themselves over some period of time); (3) a global or macro level (there is some property of 'wholeness'); (4) it is the product of a dynamic process (it evolves); and (5) it is 'ostensive' (it can be perceived). For the purposes of this book, emergence teams are focused on operationalizing the Cynefin framework discussed in this chapter, and the designation 'emergence team' is justified as explained in the following paragraphs.

As the following paragraphs will make clear, emergence teams are consistent with the process as defined above in Wikipedia (2015). Snowden (2005, p. 45) advanced what he described as 'a new simplicity in decision-making' based on multi-ontology sensemaking. Snowden (2005, p. 45) further defined multi-ontology sensemaking as being about understanding when to use 'both the structured, ordered approach based on planned outcomes, and the un-ordered emergent approach focused on starting conditions'. Snowden (2005, p. 45) proposes, as an example of multi-ontology sensemaking, the organization of a birthday party for a group of young children. Prior to the party there would only be a general sense of what the party should look like. Fixed objectives related to the children's learning and achievements would not be part of the plan, but rather a structure would be created to exclude such things as unacceptable behaviour. However it would be planned that party games and so on would be arranged to encourage formation of self-organized party interaction. At the end of the party it would be clear whether the party had been a success, but it would have been impossible before the party to define in specific terms what that success would look like.

We have already noted earlier in this chapter that we recommend using Snowden's (2014) Cynefin framework when addressing significant organizational problems, especially in VUCA environments. We further believe that a multi-ontological sense-making approach matches well with this framework, and this approach is the one that we recommend for application by the emergence team. In Chapter 2 we describe how a certain amount of structure is provided for the team from the team sponsor's written guidance, but then in later dialogue with the team leader and potentially the team members, the team's final objectives are emergent. Furthermore, as described in Chapter 3, the actual formation of the team and the selection of its members and individuals who are to be interviewed by the team are made as a result of whole-organization crowdsourcing (Brabham, 2013). In other words, the make-up of the team and its sources of information for making meaning are emergent. Finally, the narrative related to the problem that the team eventually articulates cannot be defined in specific terms before it is written since it will emerge based on the stories related by the interviewees, and the skills of the interviewers, and the emergent action learning process by which all these elements are brought together. If the team has authority to move into the 'probe, sense, respond' phase of the Cynefin framework it is quite possible that new individuals with special practical skills relevant to this phase may be added to the team. This too will be an example of emergence. In this chapter we recommended the use of action learning throughout the various phases of the Cynefin framework. The end results of action learning sessions are emergent and depend on the deep reflection, knowledge sharing and sensemaking of all the action learning session participants. Anyone who has ever taken part in an action learning Set knows that the results are invariably surprising, as one would expect from an emergent process. For all of the above reasons we have coined the descriptor 'emergence team' to define the teams described in this book.

Emergence teams and requisite variety

In regard to how a business organizes to apply the Cynefin framework, the 'principle of requisite variety' (Ashby, 1981) becomes very important. This principle suggests that the internal diversity of any internal system must match the variety and complexity of its environment if it is to be successful in dealing with the challenges posed by the environment. Adhering to this principle indicates that to successfully categorize the environments facing an organization and to define an appropriate response or series of responses, the organization must access a pool of individuals with experience in facing the challenge(s) of the environment in question. The organization may also choose to include in this pool individuals having expert knowledge of disciplines relevant to challenges of the environment in question or who have strong networks with individuals having relevant knowledge. In this book it is recommended that to access this pool of individuals, the organization develops an emergence team, which in some ways is similar to a self-directed team. It meets together as a long-term community and is made up of employees who are fully responsible for turning out a defined segment of finished work or service. Since every member of the self-directed team is responsible for the finished segment, such teams are the opposite of assembly line teams where each team member is responsible for only a narrow segment of the finished product or service (Orsburn et al., 1990).

Emergence teams versus other team structures

In the context described above, such teams might also be characterized as 'matrix' teams, 'cross-functional' teams, or 'transdisciplinary' teams, or even in combinations of these terms, for example cross-functional matrix team. A matrix team is composed of people from different areas of an organization who are brought together to solve a common problem or achieve a goal through collaboration. Team members could also be drawn from outside the organization, for example, customers, suppliers or consultants. A cross-functional team is a team of people with different functional expertise working towards a common goal; for example it might include people from planning, IT and human resource departments. A transdisciplinary team is one in which members come together to jointly communicate, exchange ideas and work together whilst emphasizing freedom to cross the lines of their disciplines as they do so.

An exception to the above emergence team approach may well be necessary under chaotic conditions when response time is often of the utmost importance. In such cases a sole decision maker may be necessary, for example the emergence team leader, although this decision maker should try to obtain the recommendations of as many informed sources as feasible, given the time constraints.

While emergence teams have something in common with matrix teams, cross-functional teams and self-directed teams, the make-up of emergence teams is quite unique and particularly challenging since each emergence team members represents a centre of excellence that combines in-depth experience and knowledge not only regarding their own organizational domain (as in matrix teams) but also in reference to the problem with which the team is being confronted; they must also abandon their chain of command allegiances (unlike matrix teams) and their organizational unit allegiances (unlike cross-functional teams) becoming part of a new 'organization' which is the emergence team. The sense that emergence teams are self-directed teams may also be inappropriate since although they have responsibility for a well-defined segment of finished work or service they may hand over their conclusions regarding further work to other teams that then have responsibility for work completion. In other words, not only are emergence teams unique but also for team members they demand particularly unique kinds of individuals who are capable of assuming novel roles.

The make-up, formation, development and leadership of emergence teams form the major content of this book. Even when team members are widely dispersed, knowledge sharing, sensemaking and consensus building in such teams is vastly facilitated by the ability to support and extend team communication and knowledge sharing through digital connectivity (Smith and Cockburn, 2013, pp. 278–287); the specific benefits associated with different kinds of digital technology are described in Chapter 8. For this team approach to yield the necessary knowledge sharing and consensus, the organization must also have developed and promote an open organizational culture that supports strong social capital (Smith and Cockburn, 2013, pp. 272–278). Social capital consists of the stock of active connections among people – the networks of trust, mutual understanding, and shared values and behaviours that bind together members of teams and make knowledge sharing and cooperative action possible (Cohen and Prusak, 2001).

In complex environments, emergence teams may include matrix, cross-functional and/or transdisciplinary team members. The challenge then is exaggerated because of the organizational reporting lines involved and the overall diverse nature of the teams.

There are significant practical challenges that face an organization in a VUCA business context, and costly mistakes will be made if the organization does not apply an emergence team approach. The following case study illustrates such problems and mistakes. In Chapter 10 we will explain how this organization could have significantly improved its approach to its problems by adopting an emergence team approach.

Case Study: Nordica TV (used as basis for comment in Chapter 10)

Nordica TV is a publicly funded organization, founded in 1926, with 3,500 staff. The company has had dwindling audiences for its scheduled programmes over the last few years due to the rise in consumers using Internet TV. This is because these customers prefer more customized content over the traditional broadcast package. Production tools and working platforms are also in a process of ongoing change and there is development at an accelerating pace towards more mobile platforms. In addition, there are impending legislative changes to public broadcast financing that will reduce revenues. Nevertheless Nordica TV wishes to stay in business and uphold its long-held mission of being the premier provider of programmes nationally and across all three official languages.

As a result, Nordica invested in a plan for change.

A management team was formed to analyse market changes, investigate technology requirements and related matters such as staffing in the company's operations management unit founded in 2011. This is an important unit being responsible for the production tools and working platforms; however this choice was made without any in-depth consideration of the company's overall situation.

High-performing teams do not happen by chance. The managers that were selected to develop the plan were simply co-opted from various departments where their skills were not in high demand. The Operations Unit for which the team was planning was compiled from six very different departments and had over 800 employees in total. The managers of these six departments were co-opted into the team. Each had a set of diverse skills but as no systematic or structured team selection and recruitment was used, beyond co-opting existing managers, they were ill-matched. Motivation was simply assumed since the members of the team were senior managers. In addition their ensuing teamwork was carelessly developed. For example, an effort was made to improve teamwork based on a series of professionally facilitated workshops that were administered to the team members. In these workshops, the Tuckman four-stage model of team building (Tuckman, 1965) was described and applied to the team's circumstances. The Tuckman model stages are sequential, and cumulative in effect – they begin with Forming, followed by Storming, then Norming, before reaching the Performing stage of teamwork. The facilitator using the headline, 'Things we are not talking about' began the 'Storming' stage, but little of significance emerged in the workshop discussions, and no further sessions were undertaken. Thus the Storming stage was not completed and subsequent stages, which build upon and extend that stage of the Tuckman model, were not completed, and team development suffered as a consequence. In addition the team leader quit and no team activity ensued for a year before a new leader was appointed. The team did not achieve its main goal of developing a plan to address the company's problems, nor did it address issues related to the operations management unit. Squabbling and 'political' manoeuvring were the norm for the team since trust, a core element in high-performing teams, was missing. In summary the team faced a significant number of performance blockages including:

- ineffective leadership;
- incomplete exploration of the problem situation;
- limited motivation and focus on project priority tasks;
- insufficient team member skills and capabilities for the project;
- lack of collaboration and teamwork;
- the failure to complete team development;
- unclear goals and objectives;

- conscripted rather than selected or volunteered membership;
- limited openness and reflection following incomplete Tuckman stages.

As noted previously, in Chapter 10 we will explain how this organization could have significantly improved its approach to its problems based on the methods detailed in this book.

References

Ackoff, R.L., 1977. The corporate rain dance. *The Wharton magazine*, winter, pp. 36–40.

Ackoff, R.L., 1981. *Creating the Corporate Future: Plan or Be Planned For*. New York: John Wiley & Sons.

Ackoff, R.L. and Emery, F., 1972. *On Purposeful Systems*. Chicago, IL: Aldine-Atherton.

Ashby W.R., 1981. Principles of the self-organizing system. In Conant, R. ed. *Mechanisms of Intelligence. Ross Ashby's Writings on Cybernetics*. Los Angeles, CA: Seaside Intersystems. pp. 51–74.

Brabham, D.C., 2013. *Crowdsourcing*. Cambridge, Mass: The MIT Press.

Cohen, D. and Prusak, L., 2001. *In Good Company: How Social Capital Makes Organizations Work*. Boston, MA: Harvard Business School Press.

Deloitte, 2014. The 2009–11 shift indices: Industry metrics and perspectives. Available at: <,http://www.deloitte.com/view/en_US/us/Industries/technology/center-for-edge-tech/shift-index-tech/a4bd9b3adbd01410VgnVCM3000003456f70aRCRD.htm> [Accessed 11 July 2014].

Gaunt, R., 1991. *Personal and Group Development for Managers: An Integrated Approach through Action Learning*. Harlow, UK: Longmans.

Gittleson, K., 2014. Can a company live forever? Available at: <http://www.bbc.co.uk/news/business-16611040> [Accessed 11 July 2014].

McGill, I. and Beaty, L., 1995. *Action Learning: A Guide for Professional, Management and Educational Development*, London, UK: Kogan Page Ltd.

McKinsey & Company, 2014. Insights and publications, the new normal. Available at: <http://www.mckinsey.com/insights/strategy/the_new_normal> [Accessed 11 July 2014].

Orsburn, J.D., Moran, L., Musselwhite, E. and Zenger, J.H., 1990. *Self-directed Work Teams*. Homewood, IL: Business One Irwin.

Revans, R.W., 1971. *Developing Effective Managers: A New Approach to Business Education*. London, UK: Longmans.

Revans, R.W., 1982. Management, productivity and risk – the way ahead. In *The Origins and Growth of Action Learning*. London, UK: Chartwell-Bratt.

Revans, R.W., 1983. Action learning – its term and character. *Management Decision* 21(1).

Revans, R.W., 1984a. *The Sequence of Managerial Achievement*. Bradford, UK: MCB University Press.

Revans, R.W., 1984b. 'Meadium' on the learning equation. *Management Education & Development* 15(3).

Revans, R., 1996. *The ABC of Action Learning*, London, UK: Lemos & Crane.

Smith, P., 1993. Getting started as a learning organization. In Watkins K.E. and Marsick, V.J., 1993. *Sculpting The Learning Organization*. San Francisco, CA: Jossey-Bass.

Smith, P.A.C., 1997a. Q'ing action learning: More on minding our Ps and Qs. *Management Decision* 35(5), pp. 365–372.

Smith, P.A.C., 1997b. Performance learning. *Management Decision* 35(10), pp. 721–730.

Smith, P.A. and Cockburn, T., 2013. *Dynamic Leadership Models for Global Business: Enhancing Digitally Connected Environments*. Hershey, PA: IGI Global.

Smith, P.A.C. and Saint-Onge, H., 1996. The evolutionary organization: Avoiding a Titanic fate. *The Learning Organization* 3(4), pp. 4–21.

Snowden, D., 2005. Multi-ontology sense making: A new simplicity in decision making. *Informatics in Primary Care* 13(1), pp. 45–54, Available at <http://cognitive-edge.com/uploads/articles/40_Multi-ontology_sense_makingv2_May05.pdf> [Accessed 3 June 2014].

Snowden, D.J., 2010. Comment Friday 20 August 2010 4:37 PM. Available at: <http://mandenews.blogspot.ca/2010/08/test3.html> [Accessed 3 June 2014].

Snowden, D.J., 2014. Available at: <http://en.wikipedia.org/wiki/Dave_Snowden> [Accessed 2 June 2014].

Snowden, D. J. and Boone, M.E., 2007. A leader's framework for decision making. *Harvard Business Review* (November), pp. 68–76, 149.

Tuckman, B., 1965. Development sequence in small groups. *Psychological Bulletin* 63, pp. 384–399.

Waddill, D., 2004. *Action E-learning: The Impact of Action Learning on the Effectiveness of a Management-level Web-based Instruction Course*. Ann Arbor, MI: UMI.

Waddill, D., 2006. Action E-learning: The impact of action learning on a management-level online course. *Human Resource Development International* 9(2), pp. 1–15.

Weick, K.E., 1991. The nontraditional quality of organizational learning. *Organization Science* 2(1).

Wikipedia, 2015. Emergence definitions. Available at: <http://en.wikipedia.org/wiki/Emergence#Definitions> [Accessed 4 January 2015].

Chapter 2
Team context definition and consensus building

Team context definition

Emergence teams are only formed to tackle serious organizational problems, and since launching an emergence team is a significant undertaking, it should not be commenced without the understanding and support of the most senior levels of the organization. The CEO or a senior member of the executive team should drive the formation of the emergence team as well as assume the role of the emergence team's sponsor. This individual must clearly understand not only the problem but also the properties of emergence teams as described in Chapter 1, plus what results are expected of the team, its interaction with and impact on other stakeholders, and how successful resolution of the problem will be defined. This information establishes the core of the team's charter including the team's role and the team leader's role, and forms the basis for Example 2.1. The critical importance of establishing a clear role for the team will be explained in Chapter 3.

Example 2.1
EMERGENCE TEAM SPONSOR–TEAM LEADER–TEAM MEMBERS QUESTIONNAIRE

The following questions relate to the work to be carried out by the emergence team and are being sent to you as sponsor initially, and also to the team leader, and later to each member of the team. Please fill out the questionnaire and retain your responses providing one copy to the sponsor or team leader or team members as appropriate; these will be used as the basis for later dialogue between the sponsor and the team leader, and potentially with team members.

I   Why are we doing this?

- What imperatives influenced the decision to form this emergence team?

- Please describe concisely the problem(s) with which the team will be tasked.

- How doses the team's work relate to the organization's present and future strategies and objectives?

2. What will be achieved?
    - What will be the specific outcomes/results of the team's work?
    - How will the team know when it is successful?
    - In what manner will the team report its progress and results?
3. Definition of the team leader's role.
    - How will the team leader contribute to achieving question #2 above?
    - What role is the team leader expected to play in advocating plans, tasks and activities related to the outcomes to be achieved?
    - How must the team leader participate in leading implementation of the plans, and in sustaining commitment and ensuring cohesiveness?
    - How is the team leader expected to support team development?
4. Who else has a stake in the team's activities?
    - Who are the other key internal and external stakeholders (including other teams)?
    - What should be the team's relationship to these stakeholders?
5. How will the team's sponsor support the team?
    - What is the sponsor's role?
    - How will the sponsor and the team relate?
6. How will the team members be rewarded?
    - What achievements should the team or its members be rewarded for?
    - How should achievements be recognized:
        - At intervals throughout the project? Or
        - At the end of the project?
    - Should rewards be granted to:
        - Individual team members?
        - The team as a whole?
7. What could hold the team back?
    - Are there any critical constraints or barriers?
    - Are there security concerns?
    - How will all these constraints be addressed?
8. What could undermine the team's recommendations?

    It is critical that the team's sponsor, and other members of senior management, understand that the emergence team may uncover unpalatable facts about the organization's operations in relation to the problem with which the team is tasked, and that such conclusions must not be rejected unless they are seriously flawed. All too often, senior management of an organization will not countenance any suggestion that mistakes have been made, and indeed will suppress any such research based conclusions. Both authors of this book have carried out research reviews of unsuccessful business initiatives; these studies were based on in-depth interviews and stories from intimately involved personnel, and in both cases the resulting reports were not used in any organizational learning fashion but in fact were confiscated and destroyed! It will be important for the emergence team to ensure that its 'environment' (see Cynefin Framework in Chapter 1) research findings do not carry a 'blaming' tone but rather set out the team's reasons for categorizing the problem: Environment as a Known environment; a Knowable environment; or an Unknowable environment – complex; or an Unknowable environment – chaotic. However, unless the evidence for one particular environment is overwhelming, it is very likely that the team's categorization will not be fully supported by all senior executives or even all team members.

Consensus building

In normal circumstances, reaching decisions in an emergence team is not a matter of the exercise of authority, represented by 'power over' or technical/functional relevance, but rather involves reaching consensus among the team members and with the team leader in an action learning process where traditional boundaries are non-existent or are blurred. Consensus decision making may pose real challenges in an hierarchical organization where the culture promotes 'top-down' decision making as the norm. Top-down decision making occurs when leaders of a group make decisions in a way that does not include the participation of all interested stakeholders. Even if the leaders do gather input, they still do not include the whole group in the deliberation process, but rather include individuals that will agree with their views, or may be readily influenced to do so. Outcomes of 'top-down' decision making typically receive only 'lip service' since they are not collaboratively developed and there is little overall will to implement the decision(s). Individuals may also hoard important information because of complacency or anger at being ignored. Action learning recommended for emergence team decision making is an equal-voice practice that promotes dialogue and consensus building and totally rejects 'power over' dynamics or decision making. However, in an emergence team, ultimate action is still the responsibility of the team leader. This responsibility must not be taken lightly, and is normally based on an emergent consensus with the team members. Exceptions to this proviso are expected when the situation demands immediate emergency action, and the team leader, in formulating a decision, must rely on his/her/own experience or on the best (team?) information available at the time.

If the emergence team leader recognizes that he/she is operating in a top-down decision making culture, he/she must take responsibility for ensuring that the emergence team understands the fundamentals and processes of action learning and consensus building, and reassures team members that they all have an equal-voice in the dialogue and reflection processes leading to consensus. These messages must then be driven home through scrupulous attention to adherence to these principles.

We define 'consensus' as a multi-participant decision making process that involves dialogue and reflection among all the team members, the team leader, and sometimes the team sponsor, until the particular 'final' decision has typically the support of all the participants, or of a predefined majority. It has been emphasized previously that the CEO or a senior member of the executive team should drive the formation of the emergence team as well as assume the role of the emergence team's sponsor. It was further pointed out that this individual must clearly understand not only the problem, but also the consensus process, plus what results are expected of the emergence team, its interaction and impact on other stakeholders and how successful resolution of the problem will be defined. This information is fundamental to the team's charter and forms the basis for Example 2.1 above. All the parties must have an equal opportunity to air their views and an independent facilitator is sometimes used to ensure this equality.

Consensus may be defined as an acceptable resolution of a difference of opinion among group members; one that can be supported, even if it is not the 'favourite' of each individual (Consensus, 2014). Decisions made by consensus are sometimes referred to as synergistic decisions, because the group members working together arrive at a decision of higher quality than the decision they would have obtained working individually. Note that 'consensus' does not imply total 'agreement'. Consensus is not easy to achieve, but it is the most effective method of group decision making, although it also takes the most time. When a decision is made by consensus all members understand the decision and must be prepared to support it; therefore during the process, all group members must listen very carefully and communicate very effectively.

A number of approaches and processes relating to consensus building are described in Consensus (2014) including a Consensus-Oriented Decision-Making model which offers the step-wise consensus process set out in Example 2.2. The level of agreement necessary to finalize a decision is known as a 'decision rule'.

Possible decision rules for consensus vary and include the following range based on Consensus (2014):

- unanimous agreement (agreement is based on this proposal being a person's first choice);

- unanimous consent (consent given because this proposal is one that the person can live with);

- unanimous agreement minus one vote or two votes;

- unanimous consent minus one vote or two votes;

- majority thresholds without regard for 'agreement' or 'consent' (90 per cent, 80 per cent, 75 per cent, two-thirds and 60 per cent are common);

- simple majority without regard for 'agreement' or 'consent' (51 per cent);

- team leader decides.

Example 2.2
CONSENSUS-ORIENTED DECISION MAKING IN SIX STEPS (BOUNDLESS, 2014)

1. identify the topic;
2. initiate an open dialogue;
3. highlight underlying concerns;
4. develop a proposal;
5. choose the way forward;
6. develop the final proposal.

Some basic guidelines for consensual decision making have been set out by Johnson and Johnson (1982, p. 103) as follows:

1. Avoid presenting your own opinions over-strongly. Simply explain your position as clearly as possible, but then pay close attention to

the reactions of other group members, and carefully consider those reactions before you re-emphasize or restate your point.

2   Avoid changing your mind simply to reach agreement and avoid conflict. Support only those opinions with which you are at least somewhat in agreement, and accept only positions that seem to you to be based on sound foundations.

3   Encourage all other group members to get involved in the decision making process and deliberately seek out different opinions.

4   Do not assume that there must be one winner at the expense of one or more other group members, but instead search out and explore the next most acceptable alternative(s) for all group members.

5   Discuss all members' proposals at length and fully reflect on the underlying assumptions.

6   Listen very carefully to all members of the group, and request clarification of anything you do not understand clearly.

7   Avoid conflict-reducing strategies such as 'majority voting' or 'tossing a coin'.

In hierarchical organizations, any equal-voice process is unsettling for team participants in the early stages of emergence team formation. However, consensus is greatly facilitated when the foundational principles of action learning are adopted. Team performance management and team development are based on the cooperative development values that are held in common between team members. In other words, fundamentally it is based on how quickly the team matures and how well they bond together. Critically, sharing a set of core values and principles always entails shared interests, whereas the sharing of interests does not always entail shared values and principles for work processes. On the other hand, sharing information does not necessarily entail shared interests, but once again parties who have a 'worldview' in common are more likely to share information (Takeishi and Numagami, 2010). For example, action learning emphasizes and helps ensure that the issue be clearly stated and understood by all; that individuals offering statements and opinions are helped by other participants to reflect on those opinions and the reasons why those individuals hold such views; and that all the participants learn from and with each other through dialogue, the sharing of their knowledge and stories, and from the questions such sharing raises; final decisions are therefore emergent.

As we noted above, even in normal organizational team settings, where emergence teams are not involved, differences in interpretation of intent and language between the team leader and the team sponsor, or team members and the team leader, result in lack of consensus and frequently cause suboptimal and even catastrophic, results. All too often the organizational benefits that the team sponsor envisaged are not delivered. Resolving these problems begins with clarification and understanding by the team leader of the team sponsor's vision of team activity and expected results (initially presented in general at a meeting of potentially concerned individuals), and the emergent shaping of these intentions given the practical experience of the team leader.

This process must produce consensus between the team's sponsor and the team leader regarding the team's role, the team leader's role and the team's working context. An excellent practical consensus building process for resolving any potential mismatch is to have the sponsor fill out in detail a questionnaire similar to that shown previously in Example 2.1. When the sponsor is not a single individual, for example when the sponsor is a management committee, detailing this questionnaire forces the various individuals to reach consensus with regard to the emergence team's anticipated performance and so on, and obviates or reduces later bickering among all concerned which could otherwise result in suboptimal performance. The team leader, to the extent she/he is able, also completes the questionnaire. In a final phase, the sponsor and the team leader exchange their completed questionnaires, and after a few days during which they compare and digest the written details, they arrange to meet and reach consensus in a new questionnaire that represents their joint understanding of the team's purpose and activities. As will be explained in a later chapter, when the team leader and the team sponsor have reached consensus, a similar exercise is carried out between the team leader and the team members as a group. If this comparison indicates a mismatch, the team members together with the team leader meet together to further achieve mutual understanding and consensus regarding the team's purpose and activities. If this activity raises further fundamental issues, the team leader revisits the situation with the team sponsor and they move to resolve the issue(s). This overall process is repeated until consensus is reached between all the parties, and the final result is emergent.

Controversy and dissent

All of this activity inevitably leads to disagreements and controversy. Controversy arises when one person's ideas, information, conclusions, theories and opinions are incompatible with those of one or more other group members. Controversy is a necessary preliminary to members' attempts to reach consensus. This is normal based on the high degree of knowledge sharing and sensemaking that goes on, particularly in the early phases of team formation. A certain amount of conflict is necessary within the team to prevent 'groupthink' and numerous studies have indicated that high team performance depends on a moderate level of tension among team members. It is essential that the team leader promotes support, trust and open communication among team members if relationship conflicts are to be managed and quickly resolved. Open communication can be promoted by establishing conduct ground rules early in the team's life as described in Chapter 4, and a comprehensive discussion of conflict contexts and their resolution is provided by Smith and Cockburn (2013, pp. 51–52).

Dissent is particularly important to the development of a meaningful consensus. Challenging a particular point of view must not be treated defensively or with hostility but must be welcomed as contributing to the learning of all the participants and meaningful action. There are four commonplace varying levels of dissent:

1 Latent: when the reasons for dissent are unspoken, and suppressed doubt may surface at a later time.

2 Mild: which is often expressed through a probing question, for example, 'I'm not sure I understand', 'Could you please clarify . . . ?'

3 Moderate: ' . . . . does not make sense to me.'

4 Serious: 'I totally disagree.'

The majority of dissent in action learning centres on Level 2, and questioning is the key to effective action learning and consensus. Questions are not always intended to elicit answers but are often intended to help the presenter think through what they have said, and deeply reflect on it, and then possibly reply; a question may also be intended to encourage dialogue within the set. Questioners should use 'open' questions when possible and it is often helpful if the questioner prefaces their question with an indication of the information they are looking for. Weinstein (1999, p. 113) lists examples of helpfully phrased questions:

- To clarify – 'Are you saying that . . . ?'
- 'Could you explain that more clearly for me?'
- 'You said . . ., if that's the case what would happen if . . . '
- 'I understand what you are saying is . . . '
- 'Have you ever considered . . . ?'
- 'What do you feel most challenged by?'
- 'What happened next?'
- 'Are we asking helpful questions?'
- 'What does everyone else think about that?'

Empowering constructive dissent is one of the responsibilities of the emergence team leader. This empowerment encompasses many of the kinds of intrinsic rewards required to motivate other aspects of teamwork. There are many ways (both highly technologically dependent as well those which are less technology-reliant) by which leaders can empower and encourage employees to become creative, collaboratively involved and innovative. De Jong and Hartog (2007) for instance, found what they saw as 13 key leadership behaviours that enable empowerment of followers. As Goldsmith (2010) stated, a leader alone cannot empower someone to be accountable and make good decisions. The team members must empower themselves in the consensus building process, and management must encourage and support the decision making environment that the team inhabits.

Empowerment

Team leaders can facilitate empowerment of team members in a number of key ways. That is by devolving power to those who have demonstrated that they have the capacity to handle it; by creating a favourable environment in which people are encouraged to openly voice their concerns and openly pose challenges to 'orthodoxy', and which sustains and enables them to grow their learning and recognizes that people seek some autonomy and a sensible level of discretion over their tasks and resources in the workplace.

Empowering leadership behaviours also have to be embedded within a consensual system to deliver best effect and outcomes for organizations and emergence teams. Determining the focus of attention and ensuring capability are two key fields involved but these need to be reinforced with the will to follow through on changes and manage the dynamics as far as possible. Some sorting out of formal and informal team rules, values, expectations and responsibilities is needed in the first instance, along with regular and ongoing review and evaluation as the team and tasks evolve over time.

Illustrative vignette

Eraut and Hirsh (2007) refer to Pissarro et al.'s (2001) study of 16 US cardiac surgery departments as a useful study of collaboration and learning in cross-professional teams. Each team was charged with implementing the same process. This involved utilizing a new technology for minimally invasive cardiac surgery. Compared to conventional surgery, the new procedure was 'a far more integral process in which task boundaries are more blurred and tasks are more interdependent. Thus, the technology disrupted the smooth flow of the [conventional] operating routine and required the development of new communication behaviors to enable the execution of a more interdependent set of processes'.

Consensus was reached that the key outcome benchmark to be used was the 'net adjusted procedure time', after subtracting the period of 'aortic occlusion'. Doing that meant that the only significant variation was the doctor's speed, rather than that of the team as a whole. Faster times both improve patient safety and save money. All teams attended a three-day training programme before starting their first case. By the time of their 40th case, the fastest team's adjusted procedure time was 143 minutes whereas the slowest team took 305 minutes. The average time was 220 minutes.

There were no changes of team members for the first 15 cases, and after that new members had to observe four cases and be mentored through two cases before being fully admitted to the group. The surgeon encouraged input and feedback from other team members in the operating room, and was described as 'willing to empower the team'.

The key factors accounting for the variations were:

1. the fastest team was handpicked by the team leader (the surgeon using the new procedure);

2. team members were picked on the basis of their previously demonstrated ability to work well together (rather than their seniority); and

3. ongoing attention to the learning of the team and the coordination with the other relevant departments.

Further exploration of consensus

Emergence teams in VUCA contexts complete tasks that have more than one possible solution or they perform under a flux of rapidly shifting constraints, shortening time horizons and fluid boundaries and decision parameters. Therefore, they are called upon to be highly agile and innovative in reaching consensus, in order to be adaptable to both the ill-defined tasks they have to fulfil as well as in their responses to continuous changes in the task environment.

In order to find solutions and make decisions in an emergence team, individual members, including the team leader, must be willing to pool information and consider different viewpoints. Team members seldom share the same point of view about every idea or issue that crop up. Polarized views, cliques and 'die hard' resisters can often block the progress of a team. Teams generally seek or may be pressurized to speedily get members to come to a consensus and begin to focus on both what their goal is and how it is to be achieved as well as how to tackle any emergent issues. Some types of teams or workgroups can reach a consensus quickly and others ignore this and simply continue to engage in their typical professional or disciplinary roles.

There must be clarity and openness of discussions (without fear of repercussions from leadership) in order to make sure everyone understands the project, goals, idea or issue, and how consensus will be reached, whilst still confirming areas of explicit disagreement or doubt (van Cleef et al., 2010). Such transparent discussions will necessarily invoke some degree of negotiation as to the extent of dissenters, withholding of agreement or of willingness to accept the majority opinion. In respect of 'hearing' what is being said there are some ICT tools and techniques or methods to manage or improve debate and discussion so that the team members hear and understand/discuss all the different sides to a discussion or negotiation of a consensus (Beers et al., 2006).

Of course, when there is a lack of trust, or the team is new, there may be some reluctance to openly voice criticisms or doubts. One approach for leaders is to get anonymous feedback; allow a 'cooling off' period for reflection for all; or adopt a mediator role. Naturally there are costs, such as time-to-action agreed proposals, possibility of 'political' forms of action and potentially extra fees or resource costs in such methods if dissenting voices are ignored, bullied or otherwise threatened. As a result the team sponsor or team leader may have to remove dissenters in extreme cases if they sabotage or undermine the rest of the team's efforts.

Successful emergence teamwork outcomes emerge from all such complex dynamic interplay of many different inputs and processes along with cognitive maps of key knowledge. These include team narratives of boundary closures or interface dynamics between significant players in the unfolding action. However, there are various levels of what could be called 'intentional' team action; some of it is explicit and well-articulated, and the other actions are tacit and unarticulated.

> *Much knowledge – including many practical applications – is tacit, or embedded in specific social networks with their largely unquestioned routines; indeed, these networks are often creating and recreating knowledge, rather than simply engaging in a series of one-way knowledge transfer.*
>
> (Field, 2006, p. 13)

Some actions by people are unconscious habits, or intuitive and/or 'unknown', whilst others form part of the complexity of the richly interactive social systems people inhabit and develop through action learning, and which teams confront in the four Cynefin environments detailed in Chapter 1. Some forms of team action may then provide unintentional gains initially; however if grasped and successfully integrated into the team's practical approach to problems and issues, they will have a tangible and explicit impact on events, processes and systems and also on the leeway or 'affordances' these systems and actions enable (Cook and Brown, 2002).

These affordances involve the emergence of intertwined cognitive and emotional states in the team. Individuals in teams sometimes neither share each other's grasp of the systems nor their own roles in the team. Sometimes, some team members may perceive leadership input, such as the system designated for their empowerment, as being unsatisfactory. A lack of team consensus may then create or magnify the problem, or diminish confidence and morale amongst all the team members. A strong team consensus, on the other hand, typically promotes shared values, and prevents problems emerging, or at least diminishes their impact. Such consensus is promoted by pursuing the sponsor/team leader/team members' dialogue generated as discussed above in relation to Example 2.1. However, no amount of effort can wholly prevent misunderstandings. Individuals often shift in their allegiance to agreed aims and concerns unexpectedly, or as a result of a spontaneous interaction with others; this is a further example of emergence. As highlighted in Chapter 1, surprise is the new norm in the VUCA environment that organizations face today, and even the seemingly tightest of consensus regarding team matters should be viewed as 'provisional'. In order to confront habitual or routine approaches to self-knowledge as much as to delineate technical forms of knowledge embodied in the team, action learning and deep reflection are mandatory. Some of the above unintentional dynamics are more noticeable to new members and thus the entry-stage for these people may involve learning for the *whole* team and perhaps a new consensus (Cockburn, 2005; Smith and Cockburn, 2013; 2014).

The consensus and the clarity of understanding and agreement on the project scope and terms between team leader and team sponsor must also be supplemented with clarity about the current or anticipated team morale whilst undertaking their work; an important factor with regard to team efficacy. One of the factors most significantly impacting team morale and causing disagreements invariably involves how, or if, team members, or the overall team itself, will be rewarded for performance. For example:

- What achievements should the team or its members be rewarded for?

- When should achievements be recognized:

    - At intervals throughout the project? Or

    - At the end of the project?

- Should rewards be granted to:

    - Individual team members?

    - The team as a whole?

As noted in the questionnaire in Example 2.1, these questions should be resolved as the team's context is defined, since they have the potential to impact 'Interpersonal trust'. Calinog (2014) asserts that 'Interpersonal trust' is an enormously important factor in ensuring a team meets its goals. 'Interpersonal trust' is defined as 'an individual's belief that another individual makes efforts to uphold commitments, is honest, and does not take advantage given the opportunity' (Ferrin and Dirks, 2003, p. 19). 'Interpersonal trust' is built as interdependent members of the emergence team collaborate in a wide variety of ways (Ferrin and Dirks, 2003; Rousseau et al., 1998) and especially when there is a significant element of risk involved for team members with no guarantee that other team members will reciprocate (Ferrin and Dirks, 2003).

Barriers to collaboration and reward systems

Barriers to collaboration that most frequently occur, to some extent, in all teams include ineffective technology, legacy systems, bureaucratic processes and other procedures that hamper progress. Limitations in effective allocation of resources such that there are perceived gaps between what is provided or accessible and what is required may lead to self-fulfilling negative outcomes. Beyond the above-mentioned factors such things as a lack of equitable incentives and rewards for all collaborators, or individualized incentives rather than group incentives, may subsequently build resentment and conflict.

Within the rewards category, other matters such as the accessibility and restrictions upon the numbers, levels or types of contributors sharing in the rewards may cause resentment. For example, restrictions on who gets recognition such as promotions, or who is qualified to get bonuses or to access professional development, often build a sense of injustice amongst the excluded. These negative situations are further compounded if there is no transparency, a lack of candour or carelessness in the communication about rewards. The most commonly heard disadvantage of whole-group/team-based rewards is the so-called 'free-rider' phenomenon.

One prime concern for members of an emergence team is the nature of the rewards system operative within the Cynefin framework. Rewards need not always be financial, such as bonuses, or highly visible, such as being promoted. Templer et al. (2010) suggest that the motivational power of financial rewards varies for different groups of employees. Empowerment with constructive feedback, praise and coaching or mentoring and creative or intellectually challenging projects may instead be sought as a reward or may be expected as part of a rewards package by ambitious professionals. Calinog (2014) states that many organizations have found that implementing a reward system for employees who demonstrate successful teamwork provides great synergy, but Bolch (2007, p. 91) stresses that such a system 'must be carefully structured to avoid unintended consequences that could undermine individual initiative and business goals'.

Conventional wisdom suggests that team-based pay reward is the best way to encourage cooperation (Merriman, 2008). When team members are highly interdependent and must rely on each other for support or information to reach their desired goals, they are more likely to realize the value of team rewards. Consistency is essential and the establishment of objective, fair processes and measurable rewards criteria will be closely linked to the success and acceptance of team-based rewards (Calinog, 2014). In addition, cooperation amongst team members is often enhanced by the teams' perception of fairness, which 'starts with an allocation of rewards that members consider equitable' (Merriman, 2008, p. 32). We consider that the emergence team sponsor should make the reward-justification decisions when a team-based pay reward has been adopted, and that the emergence team leader should make the reward-justification decisions when an individual team member system is in use.

References

Beers, P.J., Kirschner, P.A., Bosschuisen H.P.A. and Van den, Gijselaers, W., 2006. Common ground, complex problems and decision making. *Group Decision and Negotiation* 15(6), pp. 529–556.

Bolch, M., 2007. Rewarding the team. *HR Magazine* 52(2), pp. 91–93.

Boundless 2014. Techniques for reaching consensus. Available at: <https://www.boundless.com/management/textbooks/boundless-management-textbook/decision-making-10/managing-group-decision-making-81/techniques-for-reaching-consensus-391–4738/> [Accessed 20 November 2014].

Calinog, C., 2014. Available at: <http://www.sesp.northwestern.edu/masters-learning-and-organizational-change/knowledge-lens/stories/2011/team-based-rewards.html> [Accessed 20 December 2014].

Cook, S.D.N. and Brown, J.S., 2002. Bridging epistemologies: The generative dance between organizational knowledge and organizational knowing. In Little, S., Quintas, P. and Ray, T. eds. 2002. *Managing Knowledge*. Thousand Oaks, CA: Sage.

Cockburn, T., 2005. Communities of commitment: Leadership, learning spirals, teamwork and emotional regimes on an MBA team, 1997–1999. Unpublished Doctoral Thesis.

Consensus 2014. Consensus decision-making. Available at: <http://en.wikipedia.org/wiki/Consensus_decision-making> [Accessed 20 November 2014].

De Jong, J.P.J. and Den Hartog, D.N., 2007. How leaders influence employees' innovative behavior. *European Journal of Innovation Management* 10(1), pp. 41–64.

Eraut, M. and Hirsh, W., 2007. The significance of workplace learning for individuals, groups and organisations, SKOPE Monograph 6. Oxford: Pembroke College.

Ferrin, D.L. and Dirks, K.T., 2003. The use of rewards to increase and decrease trust: Mediating processes and differential effects. *Organization Science* 14(1), pp. 18–31.

Field, J., 2006. Social networks, innovation and learning: Can policies for social capital promote both economic dynamism and social justice? Available at: <http://www.obs-pascal.com/> [Accessed 17 November 2007].

Goldsmith, M., 2010. Empowering your employees to empower themselves. Available at: <https://hbr.org/2010/04/empowering-your-employees-to-e/> [Accessed 26 May 2015].

Johnson, D.W. and Johnson, F.P., 1982. *Joining Together*. Englewood, NJ: Prentice-Hall.

Merriman, K. 2008. How trust teams prefer individualized pay. *Harvard Business Review* 86(11), p.32. Available at: <*www.kk*merriman.*com/uploads/*Merriman_HBR_*article.pdf* > [Accessed 4 January 2015].

Rousseau, D.M., Sitkin, S.B., Burt, R.S. and Camerer, C., 1998. Not so different after all; A cross-discipline view of trust. *Academy of Management Review* 23(3), pp. 393–404.

Smith, P.A.C. and Cockburn, T., 2013. *Dynamic Leadership Models for Global Business: Enhancing Digitally Connected Environments*. Hershey, PA: IGI Global.

Smith, P.A.C. and Cockburn, T., (eds) (2014). *Impact of Emerging Digital Technologies on Leadership in Global Business*. Hershey, PA: IGI Global.

Takeishi, A. and Numagami, T., 2010. Boundaries of innovation and social consensus building: Challenges for Japanese firms. In Itami, H., Kusunoki, K., Numagami, T. and Takeishi, A. eds. 2010. *Dynamics of Knowledge, Corporate Systems and Innovation*. Berlin, Germany: Springer-Verlag.

Templer, A., Armstrong-Stassen, M. and Cattaneo, J., 2010. Antecedents of older workers' motives for continuing to work, *Career Development International*, 15(5), pp. 479–500.

Van Kleef, G.A., Homan, A.C., Beersma, B. and van Knippenberg, D., 2010. On angry leaders and agreeable followers: How leaders' emotions and followers' personalities shape motivation and team performance. *Psychological Science*, 21 pp. 1827–1834.

Weinstein, K., 1999. *Action Learning* (2nd Ed.) Aldershot, UK: Gower.

Chapter 3
Establishing an emergence team

Background

In today's chaotic business climate it is to be expected that managerial and general employee rigidity and faith in authoritarian control will rise with the feelings of insecurity and uncertainty associated with a major organizational problem, although such faith is largely misplaced. What are needed are 'authority' relationships in the organization not 'authoritarian' relationships. In 'authority' relationships the 'supervisor', in this case the team sponsor, as explained in Chapter 2, sets the boundaries and context for the team's work. As described in Chapter 2, the supervised individuals, that is the team leader and team members, have the right to negotiate changes in the boundaries. This is an example of both emergence and empowerment! Lack of control is counterproductive – if the team sponsor abdicates this responsibility, team development and overall results will suffer as team members become more rigid and are made to feel responsible for tasks and outcomes that they cannot control; however the sponsor must take care in outlining the project framework not to become too inflexible in negotiations with the team leader and potentially with team members.

Emergence teams are normally only formed to tackle serious organizational problems. In view of the onerous nature of such an undertaking, it will promote organizational buy-in if the CEO initiates the formation of the emergence team and ensures that all senior executives and managers clearly understand not only the problem but also what results are expected of the emergence team, and in particular how it will be established. As suggested previously, a senior executive should assume the role of team sponsor. The impact of the team's activities on the organization's day-to-day activities will probably be significant and should also be explored, in order to obtain general management support. Senior management must instruct all departments to relieve the team leader and team members of all their normal organizational priorities and duties when the teams are officially identified, and to collaborate with the emergence team as necessary. It should also be made clear to units across the organization that they must facilitate the interview phase of the team's activities by releasing interviewees promptly when requested. The sharing and discussion of these preliminaries should be carried out in one or more senior-level meetings prior to the general organizational announcements. Furthermore, as explained in Chapter 2 it is critical that the team's sponsor and other members of senior management understand that the emergence team may uncover unpalatable facts about the organization's operations in relation to the problem with which the team is tasked, and that such conclusions must be accepted unless they are proven seriously flawed.

It is also very important that senior management make the decision to initiate an emergence team as soon as the major organizational problem is identified

The following descriptive points may prove helpful to senior managers envisaging an emergence team:

- Emergence teams address serious multi-dimensional, organization-wide strategic problems and issues in VUCA contexts, where developing shared narratives as input for the team's sense-making processes are vital but where such narratives are often extremely fragmented in the far-from-equilibrium periods these teams inhabit and sensemaking is critical to the team's success.

- Emergence teams are formed to operationalize the Cynefin framework (Chapter 1).

- Emergence teams are best established via the organizational recruitment and selection process detailed in this chapter.

- Emergence teams progress very rapidly to the Performing stage and thus deliver results very quickly.

- Emergence teams are made up of a small number (usually six) of highly competent knowledgeable individuals capable of deep reflection and sensemaking with excellent interpersonal and problem solving skills.

- Emergence team members are self-starting, well-trusted, widely networked, tech-savvy professionals, who use carefully developed interview skills in establishing a problem narrative and open, participative problem solving processes with their team colleagues and across their boundary-spanning networks to define appropriate (emergent) responses.

Note: only the first four points in the above list should be used in the general organizational meetings since the last two points may unduly influence the team nomination process by mistakenly indicating that management is seeking a specific archetype.

Team formation

The process recommended for the formation of the team is described below.

It causes some disruption in normal routine, and team activity as noted previously disrupts accepted lines of command and traditional reporting mechanisms. In addition, since team members will almost certainly not be performing their traditional duties, additional overhead costs will be incurred. The whole organization must understand and acknowledge that the formation and activities of an emergence team are serious priority organizational initiatives. Preferably, all formal communications in regard to an emergence team should be signed or counter-signed by, for example, the CEO or the team's sponsor.

Many issues can arise if the official processes of team organization or identification of the team or its leader are opaque or ill-managed during the communications stages, especially with respect to the team's purposes, goals and rewards. Such failures may lead to, or indeed worsen, other issues, such as insufficient employee input during team sourcing. Sometimes the team itself causes issues through informal or tacit productivity ceilings that they impose on their work. This is caused by emotions related to interpersonal events that arise during team formation causing some team members to adopt a limit to their activities.

A 2005 Watson Wyatt Worldwide study found that companies perceived by their staff to have high integrity – based upon their staff members' assessments of senior management team's trust-determining behaviours such as open communication, consistency of actions, fairness and so on – generated good financial returns. These returns were well in excess of the cost of capital investments and twice those of companies perceived to have low integrity levels. Emergence team members have to feel that their 'psychological contract' has been fulfilled by the organization in order to generate 'commitment' and encourage them to 'go the extra mile'. This is 'commitment performance' which arises when an employee's needs are fully met, and when their self-image is positive.

In addition to contributing towards enhanced productivity, 'commitment performance' appears in a number of other areas of organization and team behaviour, such as improved punctuality and reduced absenteeism. Given commitment performance, team members will also exhibit more 'pro-social' behaviours towards colleagues and customers, more ethical behaviours and will spontaneously act as unofficial emergence team ambassadors.

Network analysis

The temptation to pick the team leader, team members or potential interviewees utilizing formal Network Visualization & Analysis (NVA) or formal Social Network Analysis (SNA) by asking a series of questions of organizational employees (Smith, 2005) must be resisted for the reasons highlighted below. Of these two methods, in other circumstances, NVA would be the more appropriate choice since the principle focus of NVA (Smith, 2005) is to identify people who are formally and/or informally influential according to a given criteria or descriptive archetype, for example formal and informal leaders; content experts; and innovators. SNA on the other hand is primarily intended to elucidate the current characteristics of a network, for example actors' roles, information flows, vulnerability, segregation and so on (Smith, 2005). Snowden (2005, p. 556) has pointed out that there are a range of critical issues in using SNA to produce objective data:

- The individual as a personality is confused with that of the individual's role or function.

- The context in which the analysis questions are posed or answered influences the nature and consistency of the responses.

- Elaborate analytical constructs are built on the basis of the data derived from the questions posed on the assumption that the answers to these questions are accurate and honest.

NVA also is not wholly free of these same drawbacks noted by Snowden, and the mathematical formality (typically specialist designed and delivered projects) of the processes of NVA and SNA tend to reduce overall organizational understanding, interest and buy-in.

Another approach that must be resisted is to apply SNA to sets of employees' e-mail data (Wilson and Banzhaf, 2009) on the assumption that such data reflect operative social networks from which team leaders or team players may be derived. In the Wilson and Banzhaf (2009) study the e-mail datasets were relevant to the topic of analysis; however most social scientists would agree that in the majority of organizational e-mail cases, relevance to the topic of analysis is likely very difficult to prove, and no amount of elaborate statistical manipulation may overcome these problems.

Story-based team formation

Snowden (2005) suggests that the best way to locate candidates to carry out problem exploration (in our case the team leader and team members) is to collect stories from organizational sources; from these stories candidates (archetypes) emerge or may be derived. This is inevitably quite a slow process, and we recommend using 'crowdsourcing', where all members of the organization form the crowd. We contend that this process largely achieves the results that Snowden intends but achieves them more expeditiously.

Crowdsourcing-based team formation

Coined in 2005, the word 'crowdsourcing' can apply to a wide range of activities (Wikipedia, 2014), but in the case of an emergence team's formation, crowdsourcing pertains to a general search for answers/solutions. Crowdsourcing (Brabham, 2013) has become a popular way to gather advice and answers for businesses and entrepreneurs, and many businesses seek the advice from online communities, internal staff, and forums of all kinds to find a solution for their problems. Crowdsourcing is a cheap and effective way to gain advice and answers – by an organization going to the community of its regular employees for inputs, the organization has a wide range of knowledgeable people to help to find a solution. In addition this is an excellent means for gaining the understanding and enthusiastic buy-in of the whole organization for the emergence team intervention.

Team formation: detailed mechanism

Based on the above discussion, the following mechanism for emergence team formation is recommended:

> STEP A: Immediately prior to carrying out the nomination/selection process described in 'B' below, one or more general organizational meetings are held to acquaint all the organization's staff with senior

management's decision to form an emergence team to address a significant organizational problem. The problem with which the team will be tasked and any underlying issues are described together with a description of the process (see 'B') for formation of the team to tackle the problem. The team process will also be described, but not, as noted above, the personal characteristics of the team leader or team members. The reward for the team or a team member on completion of the team activity is also described at this general meeting. The crowdsourcing process described here and in STEP 'B' involves every member of the organization nominating an individual for the position of team leader and nominating a second individual as a team member based on the nominator's judgement that these individuals will have something to contribute to the team based on the nominees' expertise or knowledge. Two additional individuals will be nominated for interviews; these individuals will be interviewed in due course to recount to team members' stories illustrating the history of the problem or other pertinent information or background knowledge that they possess.

STEP B: Essentially concurrently with step A, the organization's IT department develops and installs:

a) 'Crowdsourcing' software to allow every member of the organization to submit from their PC or mobile device four names of organizational employees into a database specifically set up to hold these names – one name is nominated for team leader and the second for team member and the two other names are candidates for interviews by team members to ascertain stories illustrating previous 'history' of the problem.

b) Software to process the database of names to output to a designated senior individual, for example, team sponsor (and later to the team leader), the list of names ordered by frequency of appearance in the database; note that the top 10 most frequently cited names for team leader, and top 20 for team member will normally suffice in those categories.

In this nomination process, individuals are free to nominate themselves or to not nominate anyone. The team leader appointed will normally be one of the people most frequently nominated in that category.

The problem on which the emergence team will work is typically of serious and significant importance to the organization; however, a less serious departmental problem or a problem limited to a specific product could be addressed using an emergence team based on a similar crowdsourcing approach to the one described in this chapter, but somewhat curtailed. In other words, the number of people approached to take part in the crowdsourcing exercise might be relatively small. This would be dependent on accessing sufficient numbers of people with knowledge appropriate to the problem or product in question.

Choice of team leader

The team leader in many ways is an embodiment of the team, and it is critical that the organization's executives have the utmost confidence in this individual. For this reason, we recommend that the executives, or the sponsor, choose a leader in whom they have this kind of confidence. This is because a high degree of confidence in the team leader (and the team) expressed by the organization's executives will significantly enhance the team's chances of success. The individual identified as team leader should be chosen from among the individuals nominated with the highest frequency during the organization's team member nomination process. We do not recommend that team members themselves choose the team leader from among their own ranks. It will be particularly helpful if the individual chosen has previous successful experience as a 'routine' team leader, or at least as a 'routine' team member.

It is critical that the senior staff who pick the individual to become the emergence team leader be familiar with the concept of emotional intelligence (EI), and its importance to a successful emergence team initiative. The following paragraphs are intended to make clear that EI is a critical component of a team leader's personality make-up that can significantly influence team members' behaviour and ultimately the team's success. Gleeson and Crace (2015) explain that understanding how a person's brain works and how their emotional response system functions are of significant importance when choosing a person to be the team leader. Being able to relate the behaviours and challenges of EI to workplace performance are an immense advantage in building an exceptional emergence team.

Emotional intelligence

According to Wikipedia EI (2015) 'Emotional intelligence (EI) is the ability to monitor one's own and other people's emotions, to discriminate between different emotions and label them appropriately, and to use emotional information to guide thinking and behavior'. The model of EI that was proposed by Daniel Goleman (1995) more narrowly defines EI as an array of social skills and characteristics that drive leadership performance.

Koman and Wolff (2008) refer to the work of Boyatzis (1982) who demonstrated that EI competencies (social skills) are significantly related to individual performance, both in cognitive tasks where an individual is under stress, and in tasks where many individuals are mutually dependent. Given that teamwork is a social mutually dependent activity, emotions are expected to play an important part in promoting team effectiveness. Koman and Wolff (2008) assert that teams develop a set of behavioural norms labelled Emotionally Competent Group Norms (ECGN) that shape the emotional experience in a team. Koman and Wolff (2008) further state that the extent to which a team developed ECGN had been linked to high team performance, and that their studies showed that if the team leader possessed EI it affected the team level of emotional competence and team performance and it was optimized by the development of the ECGNs.

Gleeson and Crace (2015) define EI as 'knowing, understanding, and responding to emotions and overcoming stress in the moment; plus being aware of how your words and actions affect others'. These authors further clarify that EI consists of: 'self-awareness, self-management, social awareness, and relationship management' Gleeson and Crace (2015) also affirm that EI is widely known to be a key component of effective leadership, and assert that good leaders are self- aware, and understand how their verbal and non-verbal communication can affect the team. These authors point out that one of the factors that commonly leads to team issues involves communication deficiencies which create disengagement and doubt. A leader with poorly developed EI cannot effectively gauge the needs, wants and expectations of the team that they lead. Team leaders who react emotionally without the benefit of EI will create mistrust among their team members and will probably seriously jeopardize working relationships. In other words, reacting erratically and emotionally can have a detrimental impact on overall team culture, attitudes and positive feelings towards the company and the team's mission.

To help senior staff evaluate a person's EI competencies and appropriateness for emergence team leadership, Koman and Wolff (2008) provide very detailed tables of EI-relevant social skills; however, this is more information than most senior staff will have time to deal with. Gleeson and Crace (2015) on the other hand recommend assessing an individual's EI from how well he or she exhibits the five elements listed below:

- **Self-Assessment:** this skill is based on reflection on why we make certain decisions; what we are good at and where do we fall short. Individuals must clearly understand and be comfortable with their own personality, including both their good and bad points.

- **Empathy:** is the capacity to understand what another person is experiencing from within the other person's frame of reference. In other words, it is the capacity to place oneself in another's shoes. The more an individual can relate to others, the better he or she will be at understanding what motivates or demotivates team members.

- **Emotional Restraint:** self-control is the ability to control one's personal desires in the face of external demands in order to function acceptably according to the norms of the current context. This is a critical element of EI. For example, in conflict resolution it is counterproductive to say or do anything that does not help resolve the conflict. A team leader must strive to create a positive team culture where it is acceptable to disagree but such disagreements are resolved for example by dialogue, and do not linger on as conflicts.

- **Relationship Building:** building, encouraging and maintaining healthy and productive relationships with, and among, team members is essential to generating high emotional intelligence competency norms (ECGN) in a team. A key indicator that an individual possesses this element is the quality and reach of their personal network; this may be indicated by who proposed them to be the team leader in the crowdsourcing exercise.

- **Effective Communication:** communication skills are of the utmost importance. Poor communication is a very frequent cause of problems in teams and between the team and its sponsor. Because of the exacting nature of much emergence team activity and reporting, superior communications skills are mandatory.

Choosing team members

We also recommend that the team leader be given the role of picking the team members from the list of individuals nominated by people across the organization. We suggest that team members be chosen from those individuals who have been most frequently nominated whilst having regard for the relevance of their previous team experience and technical capabilities in light of the problem to be addressed. In some very fortunate cases this may simply be a matter of the team leader choosing the top six individuals from the list of nominated individuals.

The names of the approved team leader and the approved team members should be announced to the organization only after they have been personally interviewed by the senior management sponsor and have agreed to assume their team responsibilities.

Team member characteristics

We recommend that the team leader bears in mind that, although emergence teams are formed and operate in novel ways, much traditional team wisdom applies (Parker, 1990; Tuckman, 1965; Tuckman and Jensen, 1977) as discussed in Chapter 4. The team leader needs to first reflect on the type of problem with which the team is being a tasked. This will help define the skill-sets and knowledge that the team must possess. It will assist the team leader in defining the team composition and in choosing individuals with the necessary capabilities. The team leader in choosing team members must not only consider the relevance of the individuals' technical-related capabilities, but must also consider teamwork-relevant personality characteristics. Some of these characteristics were described in a points list earlier in this chapter and others have been discussed at length in the literature (Brounstein, 2014) including:

- communicates constructively and speaks up and expresses thoughts and ideas clearly, directly, honestly, and with respect for others and for the work of the team;

- listens actively and absorbs, understands, and considers ideas and points of view from other people without debating and arguing every point;

- takes the initiative to help make things happen;

- shares information, knowledge and experience openly;

- is a member of a significant relevant trust network;

- willingly cooperates and pitches in to help;

- exhibits flexibility in adapting to ever-changing situations;

- works as a problem-solver and is willing to deal with all kinds of problems in a solutions-oriented manner;

- treats fellow team members with courtesy and consideration and is respectful and supportive;

- possesses strong interpersonal skills.

Other considerations for emergence team members include:

- familiar with action learning principles;

- experience in conducting interviews and sensemaking;

- understanding of the consensus process;

- knowledge sharing and sense-making aptitude;

- sound mental models of the organizational environment where the problem exists.

The team leader should bear in mind that potential team members will behave and learn in individual ways during team activities, and that in choosing team members, achieving team balance must be a concern, given the problem the team is tasked with. Individuals exhibit four behavioural learning styles (Honey and Mumford, 1992) that predispose them particularly for different stages of the action learning (team) process. 'Activists' learn best from relatively short tasks and exercises; they do not learn well in situations involving a passive role such as listening or reading. 'Reflectors' learn best when they are able to stand back, listen and observe; they do not learn well if they are rushed and have no opportunity to plan. 'Theorists' learn best when they can review things, for example from models or in theory; they do not learn well from activities where this is not included in the design. 'Pragmatists' learn best when there is an obvious link between the subject matter they are dealing with and the problem itself; they do not learn well from events which seem distant from the problem situation. Given that much of the team's work will be involved in interviewing to obtain stories from which problem-relevant theories may be derived, the team leader might concentrate on picking team members from reflectors, theorists and pragmatists. A version of the questionnaire that could be used to help establish the behavioural learning styles of potential team members is available online at (HoneyMumford, 2015).

Team workgroups and members' needs

According to Arrow et al. (2000) there are three main categories of workgroups. These are task forces, crews and teams. The interpersonal and work dynamics of each is different. The individual's motivations and affiliations vary in each of the three workgroups. Consequently, specific projects, tasks and activities will result in different responses. In order to effectively undertake a Cynefin framework-related workgroup (the emergence team), it is important to be able to ensure an appropriate match between group members' needs for affiliation, power, resources or achievement and activities undertaken. The team leader when chosen should take some time to become familiar with the three main types of workgroups.

1. *Task forces* are short-term, project groups, which do not usually stay together after their assigned task has been completed. In task forces the people are task-oriented and the project task determines the disposition of group members and activities engaged in by each (Arrow et al., 2000, p. 82). Task forces follow a pattern similar to the punctuated equilibrium model of complexity with extended periods of work to meet deadlines, followed by sharp transitions, for example to new projects or new tasks (Arrow et al., 2000, p. 192).

2. *Crews* are put together in modular fashion for specific purposes and activities. In crews, the interpersonal bonds are weaker as each member realizes that they and others are replaceable by similarly experienced and qualified professionals and thus their primary identification may not be with members of their current crew but with another crew or with others who are in the same profession. Such crews must be able to coordinate and manage their roles precisely and repeatedly at short notice, sometimes in extremely hazardous conditions, but always within known or knowable limits to operate both effectively and efficiently. So, for example, surgeons often see themselves as having closer ties with other surgeons than with nurse members of surgical crews (Arrow et al., 2000, p. 84).

3. *Teams* can span multiple projects and therefore typically have a longer lifespan than task forces. Emergence teams have a mixture of the features of other types of teams as described previously. The interpersonal and professional bonds may be expected to be stronger too, though that is not necessarily guaranteed as some members even

in high-performing teams, may adopt a 'crew-like' orientation to team tasks for some or all of the projects or their work schedules.

It is clear from these categories that 'affect' is a key component of most of the core activities of the different groups, whether task-related or not. In emergence teams, very little may be needed to coordinate team members' activities, since it is likely that team members will be very experienced people who understand and adopt the organization's agreed norms and expectations amongst them.

Further team leader concerns

Some additional important issues that the team leader needs to consider when picking team members include the team's sense of urgency and the perceived need for innovation or risk taking and collaboration versus competitive behaviours, for example, information sharing with others internally in the team or externally. Related matters then include the performance orientation norms at organization and team levels, for example, time horizons, acceptable devolution of power and responsibility. The team leader should remain aware that 'specialists' could be added to the team if necessary at some later time. For example, in our current knowledge era, an important aspect of the capability field is developing evidence-based decision making tools to explore future development options. Simulation tools are available to explore 'what if' scenarios and are often underpinned by big data systems to analyse, visualize and monitor strategies (Saxena, 2014; Johansson et al., 2014). Based on results from the Cynefin framework, the team might see a potential application for simulation tools and it could facilitate their activities if the team leader had already identified one or more experts in the field with permission to co-opt their services.

When the team leader is not familiar with some of these more subtle individual characteristics in potential team members, the team leader must make the effort to assess them through informal interviews prior to making the final choice of team members.

To become really engaged in the team, team members need to feel that their 'core' needs will be met – these are sometimes referred to as team member 'temperaments' (Gerke and Berens, 2014) and fall into four general temperament categories, namely Artisan (pragmatic and willing to take action); Guardian (focuses on concrete results and team cooperation); Rational (has strategic vision and exhibits an objective approach); and Idealist (collaborative approach and possesses future-oriented vision). Gerke and Berens (2014) give examples of the kinds of input that the team leader must provide during team operation in order to satisfy the needs of these four temperaments, for example:

- Artisan: leader must 'Set boundaries and parameters early'.
- Guardian: leader must 'Define a structure for forming the team'.
- Idealist: leader must 'Recognize and affirm unique talents'.
- Rational: leader must 'Give a rationale for any prescribed processes'.

During the informal interviews that the team leader holds to gain familiarity with potential team members, the leader should try to identify which candidates exhibit the listed temperaments. The team leader may not wish to include in the team individuals exhibiting certain temperaments. Further details of the implications of including in the emergence team individuals displaying various temperaments are provided in Chapter 4.

Team size

Although team size is not necessarily the first consideration of the team leader when it is time to establish the emergence team, it is a significant early decision. Conventional wisdom (Knowledge@Wharton, 2014) in regard to optimal team size advocates five or six team members, and we recommend that whenever possible a convergence team should consist of six members plus the team leader, unless the problem to be faced demands capabilities far beyond those of six individuals.

Chapter 4 details further fundamental knowledge that the team leader should possess and apply as team development progresses from this point.

Network stimulation

Snowden (2005, pp. 558–560) reviews the topic of network stimulation (SNS). According to Snowden, SNS is a technique that replicates the process by which informal trusted communities form. We assert that the process for establishing an emergence team, as described in this chapter, is a form of SNS. Most importantly, the process is bottom-up and not imposed top-down. In this way, a truly disparate group of individuals is brought together to address a serious organizational problem, and through their shared activity they form trust bonds that will persist beyond their team activities and throughout the organization. We further claim that even when the team is disbanded, such a network will represent a powerful learning and 'opinion leader' community across the organization with significant benefit to the organization's ability to solve intractable problems in the future. The pivotal role that opinion leaders play in furthering the adoption of innovations across an organization is described by Smith (2005, p. 569). This author argues that opinion leaders bridge the gap between innovators and the potential pragmatist early-adopters of an innovation. Although often few in number, in a sense these individuals act as catalysts for ongoing knowledge sharing. This is a valuable side-benefit of the emergence team development process described in this chapter.

References

Arrow, H., McGrath, J.E. and Berdahl, J.L., 2000. *Small Groups as Complex Systems*. London, UK: Sage.
Boyatzis, R.E., 1982. *The Competent Manager: A Model for Effective Performance*. New York, NY: John Wiley & Sons.
Brabham, D.C., 2013. *Crowdsourcing*. Cambridge, Mass: The MIT Press.
Brounstein, M., 2014. Ten qualities of an effective team player. Available at: <http://www.dummies.com/how-to/content/ten-qualities-of-an-effective-team-player.html> [Accessed 1 December 2014].
Gerke, S.K and Berens, L.V., 2014. Temperament and teams. Available at: <http://www.4temperaments.com/Models/Temperament-and-Teams.cfm> [Accessed 3 December 2014].
Gleeson, B. and Crace, D., 2015. The use of emotional intelligence for effective leadership. Available at: <www.forbes.com/sites/brentgleeson/2014/12/29/the-use-of-emotional-intelligence-for-effective-leadership/> [Accessed 30 March 2015].
Goleman, D.J., 1995. *Emotional Intelligence: Why it Can Matter More Than IQ*. New York, NY: Bantam Books.
Honey, P., and Mumford, A., 1992.). *The Manual of Learning Styles*. London, UK: Peter Honey Publications.
HoneyMumford, 2015. Available at: <www.brianmac.co.uk/documents/hmlsq.pdf> [Accessed 30 March 2015].
Johansson, P., Backström, T. and Döös, M., 2014. Visualisations of relatonics: A tool to support change in the organising of work? In Smith, P.A.C. and Cockburn, T. (Eds) *Impact of Emerging Digital Technologies on Leadership in Global Business*. Hershey, PA: IGI Global.

Knowledge@Wharton, 2014. Is your team too big? Too small? What's the right number? Available at: <http://knowledge.wharton.upenn.edu/article/is-your-team-too-big-too-small-whats-the-right-number-2/> [Accessed 1 December 2014].

Koman, E.S. and Wolff, S.B., 2008. Emotional intelligence competencies in the team and team leader. *Journal of Management Development* 27(1), pp. 55–75

Saxena, R., 2014. The analytics asset. In Smith, P.A.C and Cockburn, T. (Eds) *Impact of Emerging Digital Technologies on Leadership in Global Business.* Hershey PA: IGI Global.

Smith, P.A.C., 2005. Knowledge-sharing and strategic capital: The importance and identification of opinion leaders. *The Learning Organization* 12(6), pp. 563–574.

Snowden, D., 2005. From atomism to networks in social systems. *The Learning Organization* 12(6), pp. 552–562.

Tuckman, B.W., 1965. Developmental sequence in small groups, *Psychological Bulletin,* 63 , pp. 384–399.

Tuckman, B.W., and Jensen, M.A.C., 1977. Stages of small group development revisited. *Group and Organizational Studies*, 2 , pp. 419–427.

Wikipedia, 2014. Available at: <http://en.wikipedia.org/wiki/Crowdsourcing> [Accessed 21 December 2014].

Wikipedia EI, 2015. Available at: <http://en.wikipedia.org/wiki/Emotional_intelligence> [Accessed 30 March 2015].

Wilson, G. and Banzhaf, W., 2009. Available at: *<www.cs.mun.ca/~banzhaf/papers/Enron_CEC2009_IEEE.pdf>* [Accessed 20 December 2014].

Chapter 4
Team leader insights

Topic familiarity

It was established in the 1990s by scholars in organizational behaviour (Schein, 1992; Argyris, 1993) that there are very close links between leadership and learning, and these links continue to be emphasized today (Smith and Cockburn, 2013, p. 34). Learning in emergence teams takes place through the individual and collaborative analysis of the problem with which the team has been tasked, the encouragement of emergence, and the identification of specific objectives by the sponsor, the team leader and the team members. Given the potential breadth of the kinds of problem an emergence team is likely to face, and the wide range of relevant knowledge with which an emergence team leader must be familiar, we feel that a team leader studying only traditionally accepted teaming-relevant knowledge ensures that the team leader will take too narrow and directive a view. The critical need to be familiar with a broad range of topics is not limited to emergence team leaders being common to leaders in general (Smith and Cockburn, 2013, p. 258). A number of topics that dealt with choosing team members by the team data were addressed in Chapter 3, and in this chapter we will fill in many of the blanks for emergence team leaders.

Team leadership process

As we have asserted previously (Smith and Cockburn, 2013, p. 35), leaders in VUCA environments 'are members of a complex evolving system, where individually or in groups they are co-evolving with complexity and their own systemic contexts'. Smith and Cockburn (2013, p. 35) describe an integrated process that eases this co-evolution without prescribing the specific leadership models, behaviours, competencies and so on. In this way, utilizing their learning and experience, emergence team leaders may continually adjust their activities to address shortfalls perceived between what they are actually achieving and what their role indicates they are expected to achieve, and to promote a team climate suitable for emergence to take place

The foundation and process that Smith and Cockburn (2013, pp. 39–55) describe provides a better understanding of leadership and its development in environments such as those where emergence teams are active. This process takes into account the existing knowledge of the team leader and provides a framework to further expand this knowledge, or as appropriate, to 'unlearn' previously developed knowledge and skills that the individual now finds counterproductive. This is a process of continuous optimization and adaption, where the next leadership action is based on what is happening 'now'. In other words, leadership is emergent and is co-developed with the context in which the leadership is taking place. Smith and Cockburn (2013, p. 39) assert that, 'Now and in the future leadership is all about having a vision with an uncertain path to its achievement that may only be navigated through flexibility, agility, learning and unlearning, based on the leader's own knowledge and experience, and the collaborative wisdom of fellow stakeholders.' According to Becker et al. (2006, p. 610), 'unlearning' may be defined as 'the process by which individuals and organisations acknowledge and release prior learning (including assumptions and mental frameworks) in order to accommodate new information and behaviours'. The relevance of the above to the situation of an emergence team leader is clear, and the emergence team leader must explore the 'collaborative wisdom' of fellow team members as part of the everyday emergence team process.

Process step 1

The first step in the process recommended by Smith and Cockburn (2013, pp. 40–54) involves the team leader having excellent clarity and understanding of their leadership role – what the team leader is expected to achieve. This is the team leader's scoreboard, and the leader's success or failure will be judged by these criteria. This role will be defined initially by the team sponsor and should be finalized through careful consultation between the team leader and the team sponsor; in most instances it should be written. Given the underlying need for emergence, the role is typically divided into four related sub-elements which address the team leader's role in:

1. achieving the outcomes defined by the sponsor;

2. advocating plans, tasks and activities related to the outcomes to be achieved;

3. leading implementation of the plans, sustaining commitment and ensuring cohesiveness;

4. supporting team development.

As will be noted later, this role may be modified but any modification must not be made by a team leader without the team sponsor's agreement, preferably in writing.

Process step 2

The second step involves the team leader analysing how to successfully perform his or her role. This is accomplished using the performance system model presented in Figure 4.1. This performance model has been applied successfully by leaders in a wide range of international organizations since the mid-1980s (Smith, 1993).

In Figure 4.1 the team leader's performance is viewed as dependent on three fundamental pillars or fields (Wheatley, 1992, pp. 47–57), namely Focus, Will and Capability that help structure the leader's activity. These three elements form a dynamic system. The performance level achieved by the system (the team leader) is emergent and depends on the interactions and interdependencies of these fields.

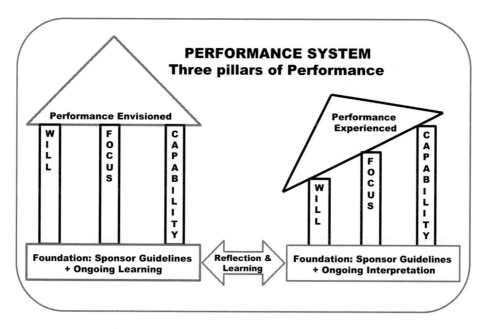

Figure 4.1   Dynamic performance system

- Focus represents a clear definition and understanding of the team leader's role performance to be achieved; Focus is associated with questions such as What? How? Who? Where? When? Why?

- The element Will represents the team leader's strength of intent to achieve the performance defined in Focus. Will is associated with the team leader's attitudes, emotions, beliefs and mindset to carry out the activities defined by Focus.

- Capability represents the 'wherewithal' to transform into reality the performance defined in Focus; Capability is associated with such diverse areas as skills, infrastructure, budgets, tools, physical assets and so on.

A change in any one of these fields may effect a change in the state of one or both of the other fields. The most favourable set of conditions for optimal performance occurs when Focus, Will and Capability form a self-reinforcing system, with all elements in balance and harmony. As the left-hand side of Figure 4.1 shows, optimal performance is represented by complete balance of all three fields. Imbalance and lack of congruence will typically lead to misdirected and wasted efforts, as well as poor performance as shown in the right-hand side of Figure 4.1.

Having only two model elements in congruence is typical of many real-life situations. For example, it is not unusual for performance to be substandard because the leader has a relatively clear understanding of the problem(s) he/she is charged to action (strong Focus), but somewhat inadequate interpersonal skills and resources to carry out the actions (moderate Capability), and no belief in the initiative's value or incentive to actualize the actions (low Will) The key to the team leader's performance optimization is the continual dynamic tuning by the team leader of the degree of congruence/balance of the elements based on the team leader's learning as shown in Figure 4.1.

Process step 3

As shown in Figure 4.2, the third step involves the team leader very frequently cycling through a succession of team-related activities in an experiential leadership learning cycle (Smith, 1999).

The team leader receives feedback as he or she compares their performance versus the outcomes defined in the role framing stage. As the team leader sees

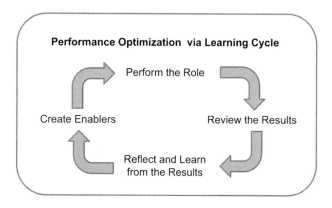

Figure 4.2   Leadership learning cycle

and reflects deeply on the results of his or her efforts, this learning provides him or her with the clues to where positive, negative or neutral influence lies. Dynamic tuning is then undertaken by the team leader to attempt to introduce or maintain congruence and balance based on this feedback. For the team leader this tuning involves 'Enablers' that are 'comprised of any understanding, knowledge, activity, capability, attitude, characteristic etc. which enables you to carry out your leadership role more effectively and better achieve intended results' (Smith and Cockburn, 2013, p. 43). Enablers are anything that the team leader feels might close the gap between role demand and role execution. It is clear that learning and reflection are keys to optimizing leadership performance.

Process step 4

Step 4 is concerned with continuously cycling through Steps 1 through 3 (see Figure 4.2) to obtain the maximum value. Argyris and Schön (Argyris, 1991) adopted the position that learning involves the detection and correction of error. Upon the detection of an error, most people look for another operational strategy that will work within the same goal-structure and rule-boundaries. This is 'single-loop learning' (Argyris, 1991) involving a simple feedback loop, where outcomes cause adjustment of behaviours, like a thermostat. This is generally the case when goals, beliefs, values, conceptual frameworks and strategies are taken for granted without critical reflection. In other words, it is the *uncritical* acceptance of a leader's role description in Steps 1 through 3 of the leadership process approach described so far.

A higher order of learning is realized when a team leader, upon detecting a mismatch between the target leadership role and reality, questions the goal-structures and rules embedded in his or her role description. This is exemplified when the team leader doubts and queries the relevance of his or her leadership role based on practical results and circumstances that he or she perceives in carrying out Steps 1 through 3 of the leadership process described above. This is referred to as 'double-loop learning' (Argyris, 1991). Double-loop learning is more creative, and may lead to alterations in the rules, plans, strategies or consequences initially related to the problem.

Emergence team stages – The Tuckman model

Traditional team wisdom does apply with regard to the number of phases or stages an emergence team will experience. The team leader should be familiar with the model advanced by Bruce W. Tuckman (1965), which has had broad practical acceptance since Tuckman introduced it, and which will frequently apply to emergence teams. However, since the emergence team must operate across the stages of the Cynefin framework (see Chapter 1) the characteristics typically defined for the Tuckman model stages may not wholly apply.

The Tuckman model proposes four stages of team development, namely Forming, Storming, Norming and Performing; a fifth stage Adjourning was added by Tuckman in 1977 (Tuckman and Jensen, 1977). For an emergence team the Adjourning stage largely consists of reporting results and reviewing the team's processes and the problems encountered; if this is done honestly, it will contribute significant organizational learning. The Tuckman model is somewhat misleading in suggesting a forward moving phase cycle, since some emergence teams may experience 'backsliding' where an emergence team slips from Performing back into Norming (but rarely into Storming). This is normal behaviour to which the team leader must be sensitive and quick to respond. Team leaders should note that because emergence teams are formed by 'crowdsourcing' based on familiarity with the excellent work, or the high reputation of, the individuals nominated, emergence teams are formed of very capable and experienced individuals who often move quickly from the Forming stage directly to the Norming or Performing stages, appearing to miss the Storming stage; this is not a cause for concern because the highly experienced team members will intuitively have reached consensus with respect to 'what, where, when, who and how' and are ready to take personal responsibility for moving ahead. If the Storming stage appears to be missed or short changed, the team leader must be very vigilant with regard to hidden disagreements and subconscious conflict.

For the team leader's information, below are the typical activities associated with an emergence team in the four Tuckman stages:

FORMING STAGE

- The forming stage should begin by the team leader and team members reaching consensus on 'How will ongoing decisions be made?' We recommend the consensus process described in Chapter 2.

- Now that the team knows how to make decisions, the team leader should lead a ground rules development session to assist the team in creating, committing to and following their own operational ground rules; such rules are particularly important for ensuring smooth running team meetings. A general example is shown in Example 4.1. The team leader should ensure that the ground rules are kept simple. In developing the ground rules the team leader might raise the following kinds of questions:

    - What kind of atmosphere do we want to create in our team meetings?
    - What expectations should team members have of each other?
    - What is it OK to do and not do?
    - Depending on whether team meetings will be held face to face or virtually, some of the points in Example 4.1 may be worded differently.

- After these opening steps, the team leader should present to team members a copy of the 'confirmed' team sponsor/team leader questionnaire (see Chapter 2); time should then be allowed for team members to digest this document and discuss it among themselves. Questions or concerns arising from this discussion should be highlighted with the team leader who must dialogue with team members to suitably address issues raised, or arrange a further meeting with the team sponsor to resolve the concerns raised.

- Next the team leader would stage a brainstorming/knowledge sharing session to facilitate creative knowledge exchange and sensemaking among all the team members with regard to the problem and the challenges that the team faces.

- The next step is for the team members to identify the team's vision and then draft a statement of team purpose and any potential barriers they perceive. Team members must next agree upon a metaphor that describes the kind of team that team members envisage they will need to form; for example, they may visualize themselves as a team of investigative journalists (Cribb et al., 2010), or an emergency surgical team might seem an appropriate metaphor.

- The team must next decide on the manner by which information will be captured. Note: Typically information will be captured via examination of existing documentation and from storytelling in interviews with the personnel nominated during the organization-wide nomination procedure; secondary individuals who have been identified during the initial round of interviews will also be interviewed and their contributions retained.

- Further team member decision making addresses:

  - What questions will be asked in the interviews? How will interview information be captured? Will it be transcribed? How will all team members access and comment on the interview information? Will it be ranked for importance versus other interview information?
  - How will team members work together? What is the team's critical work? Who does what? What are the accountabilities? How will feedback be presented?
  - How will conclusions be drawn?
  - How long are the above activities scheduled to continue?
  - Are there other barriers to the team's completing this project?
  - How does the team make improvements in its mode of operation?
  - Does it seem possible to carry out this team initiative based on the team's resources and the time available?
  - And so on.

- If feasible, in this stage team members will begin to engage in iterative cycles of information collection and storage and sensemaking.

> **Example 4.1**
> **EXAMPLE OF SIMPLE TEAM MEETING GROUND RULES**
> - everyone participates;
> - it is OK to disagree;
> - mobile phones must be turned off;
> - tablets may be used for recording only;
> - help manage our time;
> - listen to each other;
> - have fun.

STORMING STAGE

- Team members begin to engage in iterative cycles of information collection and storage and sensemaking.

- The team leader, team sponsor and team members resolve differences, concerns and so on that have arisen during the Forming stage and early Storming stage, and team members engage in the iterative cycles of information collection and storage and analysis.

- A tentative initial 'problem environment story' is prepared and ongoing activity is used to test the validity of the story and to suggest further avenues for exploration as required.

- Further consideration is given to how the team makes improvements in its mode of operation.

NORMING STAGE

- Team members engage in iterative cycles of information collection and storage and sensemaking.

- All information and sources are checked and rechecked for validity.

- A 'problem environment story' draft is prepared and ongoing activity is used to test the validity of the story and to suggest further avenues for exploration as required.

PERFORMING STAGE

- Team members engage in final iterative cycles of information collection and storage and analysis.

- A final version of the 'problem environment story' is prepared and consensus is reached on the Cynefin environment into which the problem fits and whether the recommended response should be:

    - sense (known and knowable); or
    - probe (unknowable complex); or
    - act (unknowable chaotic).

If the team has been approved to act (set out in the team sponsor/team leader questionnaire and agreement), the team reaches consensus on what action to initiate based on the response that they have recommended.

Managing team member temperaments

It is very important, especially in view of the need to promote emergence, that the team leader understands how to interact with team members. Emergence team members may be experts in their own disciplines and have formal responsibilities to various departments, which may lead to status sensitivities and divided loyalties. In particular, the team leader must understand how to interact with team members at the different stages of the Tuckman cycle. This also entails understanding the personal character of each of the team members plus the overall 'emotional regimes' teams operate within, and related factors such as the team members' 'temperaments'. These temperaments affect trust, commitment and anxiety regarding targets, objectives and goals (Cockburn, 2008).

To become really engaged in the team, team members need to feel that their 'temperaments' (Gerke and Berens, 2014), that is their 'core' needs, will be met. These temperaments fall into four temperament categories, namely Artisan (pragmatic and willing to take action); Guardian (focuses on concrete results and team cooperation); Rational (has strategic vision and exhibits an objective approach); Idealist (collaborative approach and possesses future-oriented vision). Gerke and Berens (2014) give examples of the kinds of input that the team leader must provide during team operation in order to satisfy the needs of these four temperaments, for example:

- Artisan: the leader must 'Set boundaries and parameters early'.

- Guardian: the leader must 'Define a structure for forming the team'.

- Idealist: the leader must 'Recognize and affirm unique talents'.

- Rational: the leader must 'Give a rationale for any prescribed processes'.

The different temperaments also offer challenges that the team leader must address as shown in Example 4.2.

Example 4.2
TEMPERAMENTS: STRENGTHS VERSUS ASSOCIATED CHALLENGES (ADAPTED FROM NASH, 1999)

- Artisan strengths:
    - very task focused;
    - quickly identify steps to implement plans;
    - good at dousing the 'fires'.

- Artisan weaknesses:
    - potentially impatient with planning;
    - poor prioritization skills;
    - interested in reacting rather than planning.

- Guardian strengths:
    - reliable;
    - good planners;
    - demonstrate task focus.

- Guardian weaknesses:
    - difficulty adjusting to the unexpected;
    - try to do everything;
    - difficulty prioritizing.

- Rational strengths:
    - proactive approach;
    - systemic planners;
    - conceptual-based planning.
- Rational weaknesses:
    - unrealistic prioritizing;
    - theoretical rather than practical;
    - underestimate impact of details.
- Idealist strengths:
    - knows how to get things done;
    - create plans aligned with team purpose;
    - seek a positive direction.
- Idealist weaknesses:
    - focus more on people than tasks;
    - poor on dealing with detail;
    - future-oriented at the expense of near term tasks.

It is very important that the team leader exercises a leadership style appropriate to the particular development stage that the team has reached as discussed in the following paragraphs.

FORMING STAGE

During this stage team members are the most uncomfortable and vulnerable and are most likely to exhibit their natural temperaments. Depending on their particular strengths they may become impatient with the team-building process. In this stage the team leader adopts a 'telling' style, identifying for team members the 'who, what, where, when and how'. The team leader must closely monitor and supervise the team's performance whilst providing the order and task structure.

STORMING STAGE

This stage is typically rife with conflict and disagreements. The team leader continues to give directions regarding 'who, what, where, when and how' but is prepared to hold dialogue with team members, giving explanations and taking questions. The team leader provides opportunities for clarification and conflict resolution whilst still assigning workloads.

NORMING STAGE

Here the team leader focuses on creating cohesion in the team, helping team members resolve differences and reach consensus. Otherwise the team cannot move forward into the performing stage. The team leader *shares* ideas with team members and *facilitates* decision making. In general, the team leader must *inspire* and provide *encouragement*.

PERFORMING STAGE

In this stage the team is operating smoothly, and team members are essentially 'of one mind'. Team members largely take over responsibility for decision making and so on, and the team leader motivates by promoting autonomy and trust.

Example 4.3 offers the emergence team leader the opportunity to reflect on the relevance of their approach. This Example may be used at a team meeting to obtain feedback.

Example 4.3
EXAMPLE OF SIMPLE TEAM MEETING GROUND RULES

1. How effective are your team leadership skills?
2. Does the team know why it was formed?
3. Does the team have clear ground rules?
4. Does the team have a clear written purpose?
5. Does the team have clear objectives?

6	Did you participate in setting the team's ground rules?
7	Did you participate in setting the team's purpose and objectives?
8	Do you give regular feedback to team members on their skills and accomplishments?
9	Do you collaborate with team members in defining their development plans?
10	Do you participate in the team's decision making processes?
11	Do you communicate the team's purpose and objectives to the rest of the organization?
12	Do you use the word 'we' when describing team performance?
13	Does the team know what constitutes success?

Team conflict issues

The team leader should understand that personality clashes and other kinds of conflict are inevitable between team members, and possibly between the team leader and one or more team members, and dealing with these issues will be addressed in Chapters 5 and 6. However, team performance is inevitably boosted when team clashes are reduced or eliminated. This is fostered when the members are able to agree about the extent to which they believe they have been empowered. Collective consensus (assuming it is not a symptom of groupthink) also indicates their agreement about the team's interpersonal climate and willingness to 'go the extra mile'. Lack of identity often results from team leaders' inability or unwillingness to actively or genuinely empower the team – perhaps through a tendency to micromanage, which may reflect the leader's (or the organization's) ingrained controlling tendency, personal fear of failure or lack of trust in the team. Such behaviour often impacts on a team's sense of collective efficacy too. In such cases, members don't feel mutually accountable for the team's objectives and a self-destructive downward spiral may eventuate.

The above sense of alienation among the team members often results in a number of related dysfunctional activities or behaviours demonstrating lack of commitment and being made apparent through the poor genuine effort being made by members. For instance, there may be a hidden conflict between team goals and team members' personal goals, or poor overall task collaboration. Such a climate may catalyse difficulty in reaching consensus. Team members may be rigidly adhering to their positions during decision making or making repeated arguments rather than introducing new information or using dialogue.

The team leader should be aware that emotions tend to erupt into plain sight following a period of tension and stress amongst staff in relation to perceptions of organizational justice and action-alignment. The two systems diverge when an employee maintains multiple definitions of a situation simultaneously, and the person's deepest commitment is to a private identity other than the publicly affirmed or legitimated team identity. In that case, emotion management is required to prevent the display of emotions appropriate to the private identity, and to authenticate the commitment to the team identity. For staff in all organizations then there is a continuum of engagement related to perceptions of organizational justice concerning what is acceptable as individual as well as corporate citizenship behaviour.

Thus there is a continuum of staff engagement, and unpublished research by one of the authors (Cockburn) that shows that there are punctuated equilibria within teams across their voluntary and self-organized teamwork projects, let alone in any compulsory projects or tasks handed down without consultation by the management. Consequently, there are a number of identity systems relating emotions and stories in any organization and/or team at any one time and each may interact and engage staff in more than one way as action unfolds over time. Triple impact evaluation of the impact of the emotions that emerge tends to revolve around three key questions that the team leader might pursue:

1. Is there emotional expression of positive or negative value within the frames of reference for the current emergence team?

2. Does it elevate or diminish personal or collective power and influence?

3. What is the legitimate team member response in this context?

The team leader must empower emergence team members to make choices, then validate and ratify them in action as it occurs; these decisions will then be perceived as reflecting levels of the teams' engagement.

Team leader as action/performance learning adviser

Action learning is mentioned as an emergence team process throughout this book. The face-to-face action learning process is discussed in detail in Chapter 6, together with an overview of a similar process termed Performance Learning (Smith, 1997). Both action learning and Performance Learning require a person who is not a member of the action learning or Performance Learning group to act in an advisory capacity. This person is typically (in action or Performance Learning circles) known as a 'set adviser', and his or her role is to encourage group members to maintain the principles, approach and discipline of action learning, or Performance Learning – that is to listen, question, reflect and learn, and help group members identify what is proving helpful to them and what is not. This role must not be carried out by commanding adherence to process ground rules, but rather through thoughtful suggestions and skilful questioning with the group participants in an advisory manner. The set adviser is also expected to model the kinds of effective behaviour and language that will encourage constructive working and learning in the group. In short, the set adviser 'keeps the group members on track'. Weinstein (1999, pp. 135–147) admirably details the characteristics and activities of the set adviser. In normal practice, the set adviser would be an independent consultant with in-depth knowledge and experience of the process, and this person would have been contracted specifically for the purpose.

For an emergence team engaged in action learning or Performance Learning we recommend that the set adviser role be filled, if possible, by the emergence team leader.

It would not be necessary that the team leader have in-depth knowledge and experience of the process, but rather is willing and able to assume an appropriately reflective manner in ensuring that the team members continuously demonstrate the fundamentals of dialogue, consensus building and learning described in this book.

It should be noted that Professor Revans (1982), the architect of action learning, recommended against action learning groups having a set adviser; however Smith (1998) agrees with most modern action learning practitioners by demonstrating that a competent set adviser is a necessity from a praxiological (effectiveness) point of view.

References

Argyris, C., 1991. Teaching smart people how to learn. *Harvard Business Review* 69, pp. 99–109.
Argyris, C., 1993. *Knowledge for Action*. San Francisco, CA: Jossey-Bass.
Becker, K., Hyland, P. and Acutt, B., 2006. Considering unlearning in HRD practices: An Australian study. *Journal of European Industrial Training* 30(8), pp. 608–621.

Cockburn, T., 2008. Webs of emotion: A study of the formation of team identity, 3rd Asia Pacific Symposium on Emotions in Worklife, University of Newcastle, Australia, 28–29 November.

Cribb, R., Jobb D., McKie, D. and Vallance, F., 2010. *Digging Deeper: A Canadian Reporter's Research Guide* (2nd Ed.). London, UK: Oxford University Press.

Gerke, S.K and Berens, L.V., 2014. Temperament and teams. Available at: <http://www.4temperaments.com/Models/Temperament-and-Teams.cfm> [Accessed 3 December 2014].

Nash, S., 1999. *Teamwork from the Inside Out Fieldbook: Exercises and Tools for Turning Team Performance Inside Out*. San Francisco, CA: Davies-Black.

Revans, R.W., 1982, Management, productivity and risk – the way ahead. In Revans, R.W., 1982. *The Origins and Growth of Action Learning'*. London, UK: Chartwell-Bratt.

Schein, E.H., 1992. *Organizational Culture and Leadership*. San Francisco, CA: Jossey-Bass.

Smith, P., 1993. Getting started as a learning organization. In Watkins K.E., and Marsick, V.J. eds. *Sculpting the Learning Organization*, pp. 35–39. San Francisco, CA: Jossey-Bass.

Smith, P.A.C., 1997. Performance learning. *Management Decision*, 35(10), pp. 721–730.

Smith, P.A.C. 1998. Action learning: Praxiology of variants. *Industrial and Commercial Training*, 30(7), pp. 256–266.

Smith, P.A.C., 1999. The learning organization ten years on: A case study. *The Learning Organization*, 6(5), pp. 217–224.

Smith, P.A.C. and Cockburn, T., 2013. *Dynamic Leadership Models for Global Business: Enhancing Digitally Connected Environments*. Hershey, PA: IGI Global.

Tuckman, B.W. 1965. Developmental sequence in small groups. *Psychological Bulletin*, 63, pp. 384–399.

Tuckman, B.W. and Jensen, M.A.C., 1977. Stages of small group development revisited. *Group and Organizational Studies*, 2, pp. 419–427.

Weinstein, K., 1999. *Action Learning* (2nd Ed.). Aldershot, UK: Gower

Wheatley, M.J., 1992. *Leadership and the New Science*. San Francisco, CA: Berrett-Koehler.

Chapter 5
Emergence team dynamics

Overview

Teamwork in developed and in many emerging societies today is marked by increased fluidity of interactions with others facilitated globally by the web and mobile technology (Kakihara et al., 2002). Even small start-up businesses may operate on a global as well as a local level by means of online trading or 'crowdsourcing' for instance. In *Teaming: How Organizations Learn, Innovate, and Compete in the Knowledge Economy* Edmondson (2012) says that 'surviving and thriving' today requires a 'seismic shift' in how we think about and build, collaborate or support teams.

Edmondson currently proposes using the term 'teaming' instead of teamwork, in order to indicate that this group activity is about 'doing'. The teaming skill set continues to evolve. In a 2014 working paper with M.A. Valentine (Valentine and Edmonson, 2014), she recommends 'scaffolding' techniques to support teamwork today. Such support systems apply equally well to emergence teams as to other varieties of workgroups in organizations and applies to tacit and explicit forms of knowledge and learning in teams.

Some time ago Buckley (1973) recognized the dynamic and complex evolutionary systems of team process:

> 'Process', then, points to the actions and interactions of the components of an on-going system, in which varying degrees of structuring arise, persist, dissolve, or change.
>
> (Buckley, 1973, p. 136)

Thus team 'process' should no longer simply be synonymous with static change models such as Lewin's version of 'unfreeze'–'change' – 'refreeze' since there may be many iterations of the teaming with people entering and leaving as projects evolve. Buckley also argued, ahead of many others, for greater transdisciplinary study of such temporally, as well as cognitively and culturally embodied, 'morphogenic', complex adaptive systems (Buckley, 1973, pp. 136–139).

For Buckley, varying degrees of more or less permanent 'structures' emerge in social interaction and negotiation of meaning. Such structures are: 'not only *social* structure, but also *personality* structure, and *meaning* structure. All, of course, are intimately interrelated in the morphogenic process, and are only analytically separable' (Buckley, 1973, p. 135). Thus, he implies that these are perceived as 'structures' although they are not physically embodied other than in the flow of the process or what Elias called the figuration of the 'dance' of social interaction.

The above interpretation of personality can also accommodate use of Gordon Pask's concept of a 'p' individual, referring to the corporate, team 'psychological' persona of interacting actors and their conversation. (Pask, 1976, 1980; Scott, 2001, p. 28). That is they emerge from within the relevant activity system composed of the dynamic and emotions amongst particular people, resources and places set within specific timeframes and particular organizations. Thus, these can be seen as examples of the complexity process, exhibiting a self-referential and self-organizing dynamic rather than a linear causality assumed by earlier researchers.

However, under VUCA environments, coherence is transient. As team members' views evolve alongside the team identity, and the culture or operating environment changes, so the project story needs to be 'reframed' within each new set of conditions as they occur. What might appear to be an appropriate action plan in a particular moment may be overwhelmed by events in the very near future, and the previous narrative and action plan coherence rapidly collapses into a flux at the edge of chaos. The bigger the range of viewpoints and approaches considered the better, since this avoids falling into the 'business as usual' trap in seeking solutions in a rapidly evolving market, technology or social context.

Levels of significance and performance

These social relations, processes and systems must be considered at a number of levels of significance. For example, there has to be consideration not only in terms of the relatively temporary, emergent social 'structures' generated but also in terms of the related, emergent 'personality structures' and the dynamics of interactive roles as well as the constantly-renegotiated 'meaning structures' (Buckley, 1973, pp. 148–150). That is, from the interaction dynamic and biological 'affordances' of individual personalities within the context of the team as currently constituted. The team also has a lifespan within which this action occurs, and when it may be reified as syntagmatic team action. In other words, that which is meaningful from a team perspective.

Syntagmatic refers to the ongoing interactive and conversational flow of the moment rather than a paradigmatic, (rule or norm-based) forms of action. Such action is not automatically or solely syntagmatic however. It can also be paradigmatic, when viewed as a specific 'vocabulary' relating and referring to particular team mental models, with attendant and defining norms, rules and conventions to paraphrase Blackburn's use of Rorty's term (Blackburn, 2003, p. 60).

Key norms here reflect the emergence team's commitment, trust and anxiety as regards their interactions in the project context. In order that they may be defined as meaningful such social action necessarily embodies, within its performance, the dialectical and dialogical outcomes and synergies of both the shared and the 'unshared' meanings of actors present. Sharing may be tacit or explicit in respect of how that sharing process occurs, that is, whether or not an openly reflective and dialogical process is initiated in a high-trust environment or the reverse.

Spender (1998) distinguishes between 'habitual' and 'heedful' types of performance, as do Weick and Roberts (1993). That is, between unreflexive habit and reflexive awareness (Spender, 1998, p. 21). However, Spender echoes Pask's (1980) notion of a 'p', (psychological) individual, composed of several, biological, 'm', individuals (that is, a team). To paraphrase Scott, one 'biological', or 'm' individual may 'house' several 'p' individuals (for example, as part of a role-set), and one 'p' individual may be 'housed' by several 'm' individuals (for example, as shared collective understanding) highlighting interconnectedness. In this, Spender is close to Cook and Brown's (2002) views on processes of learning and cognizing in 'communities of practice'. In fact, he states that, 'Our argument is that the most important dynamic emerges from the dialectic between the individual's explicit "conscious" knowledge, and the implicit "collective" knowledge that is embedded in the language and activities of the community of practice' (Spender, 1998, p. 35).

More generally, language and communication help define and build the common context for action learning team to operate within. Language is metaphorical and does not describe experienced reality directly but represents it symbolically. The word team is a metaphor too. Metaphors can be strung together and combined in extended configurations and descriptions compiled to reflect varied concerns, or perspectives and perceptions of the team narrators. Issues with metaphors and narratives relate to the role of the narrator as a central power to varying degrees – even where multiple 'endings' and so on have been expounded to try to show the range of possibilities and interpretations the audience may give. So a collective form ensuring polyphony of voices works best.

Experiential learning

Experiential learning is 'the way most people in fact do most of their learning' (Brookfield, 1983, p. 16). Definitions of experiential learning vary but all share a belief in the value of learners having a 'lived' (as opposed to a 'vicarious') experience to learn from in some way (Brookfield, 1983, pp. 16–19; Tight, 1983, pp. 61–62). There are many views on the appropriate epistemological, ontological and philosophical basis of such learning. Action learning and research methodologies have been employed extensively in disciplines such as nursing and education as well as management and business, particularly in Australia, New Zealand and parts of the USA, Latin America and Canada. Action Science, research and learning methods have been employed to tackle problems where ecological validity, vocational relevance and problem ownership are key concerns.

Opening collaborative conversations

Blending Schön's (1995) 'intuitive artistry' – an activated, intelligence-in-action concept – into the action learning process assists us in building an empowered community of practice amongst our co-enquirers, as we prefer to call the emergence team members. We thereby also facilitate the emergence of a self-organized form of collaborative action-inquiry and visioning. That process also serves as a complex, 'attractor basin' within emergent narratives of the community storytelling of the action learning process, practically enhancing the dialectics of individual and team agency. In the complex environment as described in Cynefin, the emergence team then codifies largely experiential knowledge of hazardous and helpful currents across turbulent and peaceful times into communal mental maps.

In emergence teams we take advantage of the potential for serendipitous 'branching out' as described by Ciborra and Lanzara (1994) wherever possible. So both scenario planning and the sharing of tacit knowledge in the team may capture any such 'branching out' and innovations. Finally, we contend that all these can be combined to empower the working communities of practice through the 'sociable' (as well as merely 'social') transformation of an emergence team into a creative knowledge cooperative. Moreover these can be combined using virtual as well as actual social space in a manner that fosters the common capture and management of diverse intellectual capital.

Emergence team stages

For the members of the emergence team, these are transitional stages transforming learning from concepts in a state of being (that) which is 'external' to the students themselves as Polanyi (1967) suggests, that is, something they attend *to* rather than something which is ontologically-embedded. In other words, something that they attend from (an awareness and knowledge of) to the rest of their actions and activity; to their being from the point of view of a conceptualization of their world as 'encompassing' the specific concepts. This transformation is the difference which they need in order to make the rite of passage from 'apprentices' to real team members; from the amateur to the professional, if you like, as in Figure 5.1. Clearly this is a communicative performance if it is anything.

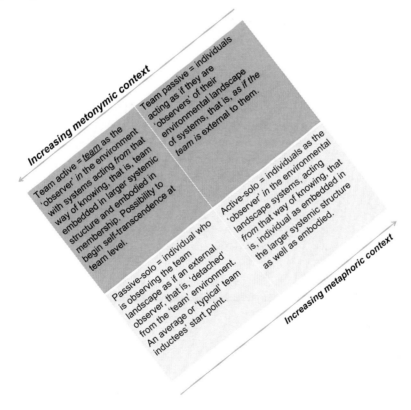

Figure 5.1   Spiral through metaphor to metonymy

We have proposed three broad fields (Capability, Focus and Will) that all leaders must act upon in teams and for the wider organization to build upon emergence in a sustainable and meaningful way (Smith and Cockburn, 2013). Meaningfulness within change emerges through an action-oriented framework of shared understandings of the 'affordances' of the embedding context and focus of the team as well as performance capabilities or skills (Cook and Brown, 2002). 'Affordances' refers to an understanding of what is 'afforded' in any given context.

Team conversations

Collaborative endeavours require various types of conversational interactions within teams, between teams and organizations, customers and suppliers. As suggested by Winograd, the 'illocutionary point of an utterance is interpreted by speaker and hearer in a background' (Winograd, 1987, p. 4). The upshot of that is that conversation is defined as more than two or three people speaking to each other. So, we do not restrict the term 'conversation' to explicit public utterances or verbal speech acts. As Winograd comments, 'It need not be a spoken conversation, or even involve the use of ordinary language. A doctor who writes treatment requests on a patient form is engaged in a conversation with the nurse who will administer the treatments, even if they never speak face-to-face. Certain requests are made implicitly on the basis of a long-term declaration' (Winograd, 1987, p. 5).

Thus, a manager does not explicitly request a full-time permanent member of staff to attend for work each morning as they have an implicit contract, which may be institutionalized in legal terms and conditions of employment. A project and the team running it may thus have an ongoing 'conversation' in metaphorical terms, about goals, resources, timelines, changing contexts and so on. Often, these implicit 'conversations' only become explicit when they are breached.

However, we must also clearly recognize the inherently unplanned character of many team conversations in VUCA environments even in those of experienced action learning teams (Stacey, 2001; Stroh and Jaatinen, 2000, p. 189; Smith and Cockburn, 2013). Implicit in this view of the character of team conversations under VUCA is the notion that each conversation is *potentially* a bifurcation or phase shift. That is, it may branch out into an infinity of complex paths and other topic areas or it may reach a dead end fairly quickly.

Team dissent

Whilst tension or dissent between colleagues in a team causes fairly obvious problems and cohesive teams are thus often lauded, excessive cohesion among colleagues may also eventually cause the decline (or the reversal of initial positive synergies) in teams. Largely this negative impact is because overly friendly teams may lapse into groupthink. In other words, there is a downside and a point at which stronger interpersonal bonds among teammates begin to lead to increasingly negative performance outcomes.

On the other hand, Guarana and Hernandez in their article titled 'Building sense out of situational complexity: The role of ambivalence in creating functional leadership processes' (2015), have proposed shared ambivalence amongst team members and leaders about projects, goals or tasks and so on, may become a functional cognitive process in some cases. Even though that situation provides much cognitive and emotional discomfort, it can also enable or encourage and promote some creative operational and strategic fluidity. That is, when there is trust and open reflection by the emergence team leader and team members about their concerns, or their varied contextual interpretation, and they exchange views and descriptions of such ambivalent attitudes.

Emotional energy and team dynamics

Trust hinges on such employee perceptions, which are being constantly updated in response to team leaders' decisions and behaviours. Many theorists acknowledge a link between a team's values and its status hierarchy, and that this thereby means that individuals who possess or adopt characteristics embodying team values are typically accorded higher status (Spataro and Anderson, 2002). This is also a key element for transformational leadership and that kind of leadership is the most pertinent for emergence teams as well as others as we have indicated previously (Smith and Cockburn, 2013).

Emotions underpin trust, affirmation and change in individuals' self-image or teams' status, influence and power relative to others. The level of energy and enthusiasm of teams for their tasks, their colleagues and their projects not only depends upon and affects the way they interact and perform but may also determine the team's longevity. George (cited in Barsade, 2003) showed that group emotions exist and affect work outcomes, amplifying or dampening the teams' trust and anxiety as they occur, thereby energizing centres of attraction across and between teams or within the them. There are four key points to note in respect of emotions in emergence teams.

Firstly, meaning-making and sense-taking in teams are interrelated. There is also corroborative evidence of emotional contagion which can potentially be measured and verified against team members and other observers' accounts

(Barsade, 2003, pp. 3–4). Rimé goes further and asserts that sharing emotions is an imperative and that this results in sharing at different levels in a wave (Rimé, 2009, pp. 71–72) which can also be seen as a means of dealing with the emotions. The two sets of accounts converge, indicating a correlation between the external observers' and the internal team members' estimations of these features. Secondly, the link between affect and cognition is a source of energy for 'dissipative structures' such as complex attractor patterns in team behaviours. Thirdly, the interrelationship between the structuring of interpersonal relationships within the teams, and how shared team emotions impact on the rest of the team's external relationship web, is also supported. This also refers to aspects of the development of social identity and transactive memory capacity within teams (Weick and Roberts, 1993; Moreland, Argote and Krishnam, 1996; Cockburn, 2005, 2008). That means including both their horizontal and vertical relations (that is, including their team level social structuration and individual team member identity). Fourthly, the link to outcomes of work, the embodiment in productive inquiry and action as they engage with the team project is important.

So the emotional dynamics of emergence teams have practical consequences in a number of ways. These teams develop diverse emotional regimes in the course of establishing their work practices and achieving goals. Such regimes may be either transient or permanent aspects of their overall team modus vivendi.

Emotional regimes in emergence teams are underpinned by both implicit and explicit sets of socio-emotional norms. This is part of what Fineman (1996, p. 218) called 'emotional rules'. These are rules of acceptable behaviour operating between people and governing how they interact with one another. They generate particular behavioural 'regimes' or 'acts and practices' regarded as being 'businesslike' in their team. These rules are also relevant to the individual and team levels of project commitment, and to values and transformations linked to personal as well as collective identity (Cockburn, 2006, 2007, 2008). In this way, emotions synchronize social interaction and foster or inhibit group unity. Inevitably, there are also emotional conflicts of interest and of practice.

Such emotional regimes emerge from the 'conversations' around the project or work activities that teams engage in as well as their organizational, professional, personal or business context. These then naturally affect their performance and the outcomes sought and achieved in these domains as well as the overall performance to some extent. Further, such regimes both reflect as well as generate the climate and overall team 'personality' as seen by observers (Cockburn, 2005, 2008, Barsade, 2003). Naturally some emotional regimes are more conducive to the individual member's well-being and to their collective well-being.

The emergence team story is thereby embodied in the project and 'enacted' in the emergent emotional regimes occurring within the lifecycle of the team and their work programmes. That can be seen reflected in the 'conversations' they have around tasks and activities, problems or issues to address and in their recounting of such matters as a narrative or report for others. A number of key factors in team development, team learning or unlearning occur through these conversations and subsequent ruminations.

Whilst recognizing the 'relative autonomy' afforded to an emergence team at various points in the team's development cycle, it is also important to recognize the interactive, interpenetrated and interconnected nature of the team's internal structuring processes. By that we mean to suggest that the individual has some level of autonomy too. That is, the individual can opt for a particular identity on the basis of their perceptions of their *individual* embedding context as well as that of their part in the team's embedding context (Worchel et al., 2000; Worchel et al., 1998, p. 55). That choice is still part of enacting team social construction; the team's 'situated cognition' about what it is doing at any time. However, team behaviour is made possible, in turn, by another bifurcation or phase shift that Oakes et al. call a 'qualitative shift' in the nature of the individual's relations with others as well as their self-conception (Oakes et al., 1998, p. 81).

Conceptualizing how teams work has used a simple model of the process as described in the Metaphor-analogy-model process described by Nonaka, (1994, 1995). A more sophisticated, multi-spiral process accounting for the interactions of individuals within a group as individuals and as a collective or a team are intertwined, though reinforcing and contending at various points and times as their 'team' story emerges or unfolds (Cockburn and Lewis, 1999; Cockburn, 2006). This approach treats teams as systems of wholes (that is, fully-formed people with agency as well as deterministic 'roles'). That is teams are treated as Complex Adaptive Systems (not subject to simple deterministic chaos like piles of sand or electric light bulbs, dominoes or snowflakes). That is, we treat them as more than systems composed of interrelated parts and avoid the reductionist error commonly associated with much earlier work (as well as much current work).

We should be clear that, as Hazy et al. (2007) state, 'Emergence in real organizations requires constant attention, support and resources, and the "success" of emergence – like successful leadership – depends in large measure on the quality of resources and attention that individuals and managers bring to the process. Self-transcendence in teams and organizations is not automatically booted up; it has to be stimulated or catalysed by actions taken internally by leaders and team members and/or external forces of change impacting on the team. The team may only have partial or even minimal control of some of these features but must be able to digest, absorb or control the good bits and eject or dilute the bad. So Snowdon's Cynefin model suits those seeking to manage these situational demands.

These authors see leaders' role as being concerned with changing local rules of engagement or norms. They also recognize the interaction between hierarchy and hierarchic ties, suggesting this can be a control mechanism for avoiding uncontrolled complexity overwhelming teams (Hazy et al., 2007, p. 30). There is no 'one best way' to achieve all of this although empowering team members is often suggested. Many traditional approaches to team building have tended to treat groups as unproblematic compilations of individuals. These groups are then disembedded and detached for training before the proposal is made to re-embed them into the former context to initiate changes developed 'outside' that system. Thus we propose action learning and deploying intuitive artistry in the emergence team. That is an enactive team construction, both embodying and embedding, through a consensual process dynamic, an empowering, 'bottom-up' approach to change and innovation.

We see the emergence team leaders' roles as about seeking ways to identify, influence or change local rules of interaction, in context, in order to encourage a positive outcome and team commitment to their tasks. We see this being in reference to the commitment, focus, will and capability fields and effected in large measure through a qualitative change in empowerment and actions on focus, motivation and capabilities in their teams. Increasingly, in the knowledge era, the cost of retention of staff is less than the recruitment costs. Some suggested estimates of recruitment costs are as high as 60 per cent of salary of the employee recruited and even higher in high demand occupations in global businesses (CIPD Annual Survey Report, 2009). Consequently, there is a drive to retain staff in many organizations as part of cost control and ensuring uninterrupted output or service.

Identity issues

Common collaboration problems in all teams relate to their failure to generate a workable team identity. There are a number of reasons for this inability to form a stable team identity. One is that there is a rapidly evolving market, organization and/or technological landscape and the team must 'hit the ground running' and make their mark in order to grab some market share. Other causes of team identity failure are the issues relating to status and roles, especially where there are strong professional identities to which some or all members adhere in multidisciplinary teams in particular. Team performance is often boosted when the members are able to agree about the extent to which they believe they have been empowered. That collective agreement (assuming it is not a symptom of groupthink) also indicates their agreement about the team's interpersonal climate and willingness to 'go the extra mile'.

As indicated above, emotions tend to erupt into plain sight following a period of tension and stress amongst staff in relation to perceptions of organizational justice and action-alignment. The two systems diverge when an employee maintains multiple definitions of a situation simultaneously, and the person's deepest commitment is to an identity other than the publicly affirmed or legitimated organizational identity. In that case, emotion management is required to prevent the display of emotions appropriate to the private identity, and to authenticate one's supposed commitment to the public identity. In terms of staff in all organizations then, there is a continuum of engagement related to perceptions of organizational justice as indicated above concerning what is acceptable as individual as well as corporate citizenship behaviour.

Committing to trust in a team and task

Building team social capital is vital to both action learning and to team bonding, commitment and trust. Social capital has been variously described but Woolcock (1999) defines it as being of three types:

- *Bonding social capital* refers to relations between relatively homogenous groups such as families and ethnic groups.

- *Bridging social capital* relates to ties across more diverse, heterogeneous groups such as friends and colleagues.

- *Linking social capital* includes ties across social strata and community members accessing resources and information beyond the community itself.

However, there remains the issue of how this form of capital can be measured and compared or benchmarked against other aspects of team performance, especially in a VUCA context. Although discussing community level social capital, Cavaye (2004) indicates some measurement is needed about goals and targets achieved/sought as well as some means of evaluating salience and impact of cognitive/affective elements such as attitudes, norms, trust and motivation. For example, in a health setting, social capital may be interpreted in terms of the social determinants of health inputs and outcomes. Such a metric must also encompass the diversity and complexity aspects, which entails moving beyond simply examining the structural elements such as how the team is formed, organized and roles within it.

Social capital is dynamic and more readily formed in a 'culturally safe' environment where there are shared values and a common purpose. This form of capital impacts and mediates the outcomes of the three fields of Focus, Capability and Will in a number of ways. For example, it impacts on relationship building, emotions and risk taking. It should be clear then that this impact might amplify or even generate some negative consequences, for example by reinforcing some pre-existing biases, unethical procedures, misinterpretations, miscalculations or misinformation in the team.

In teams it is also vital to (a) determine the focus of their commitment and intergroup trust; (b) their capabilities in terms of delivery; and (c) their anxiety or willingness to do so and to follow through as required to completion. Commitment also implies and requires some level of trust and a level of anxiety (about capability of doing a good job for instance).

Individual team members may have different 'profiles of commitment'. So, for instance, they may be highly committed to the team, but not to the organization, or committed to both, or committed to neither. Research by one of the authors has shown that commitment to a team may ensure members are willing to help each other and thus help overall team performance (Cockburn, 2005, 2008). However, low levels of commitment to either or both organization or team, often translates as increased absenteeism, team turnover or intention to leave the organization altogether.

Nevertheless, it has also been suggested that working on 'trust' is a major life project as well as an organizational endeavour (Lupton, 1998, pp. 96–97). Such life work is carried out by 'opening out the self' to others and is a general quest of everyone irrespective of gender (Giddens, 1991; Luhmann, 1986, cited in Lupton, 1998, p. 96). In intellectual tasks 'mastery is predominant whereas in value judgements or value laden times, then "connectedness" is dominant in decision-making in teams' (Smith and Mackie, 1995, p. 364). Since the tasks of an emergence team project by definition involve a mixture of these kinds of activities, in an environment of higher than average risk and uncertainty, it is perhaps unsurprising that such teams demonstrate a mix of orientations towards connectedness and seek well-attested and continuous evidence of trustworthiness within their collective. Lapses in trustworthiness are potentially disastrous, hence their tendency towards higher levels of anxiety about their team, it's efficacy and their performance, and outcomes of tasks and projects (Cockburn, 2005, 2007, 2008).

Short illustrative vignette

A brief case example in the above author's research concerned a team that had one member who was slower than the rest. In this team, there was a binary social relationship where they all converged upon concern for a member of the team who was slower than the rest, and less committed to the project, but who sought to lean on the others, particularly the team leader (Cockburn, 2006). They all spiralled around this binary at various times, weaving in and out of their positive attitudes as other attractors emerged into focus, such as the common one in all the MBA teams, that is, time pressure. Thus, it was transformed from a temporary 'point attractor' into a 'stable loop' or recurrent, cyclic attractor pattern. Such a pattern of behaviour required increased energy from them to sustain it over time within their practice as a team.

The additional energy is seen in the form of the intra-team 'emotional contagion' aligned with a 'cognitive contagion' or group emotional state of the kind earlier described by Bartel and Saavedra (2000) and Barsade (2003). These group emotions also denote not only mood convergence but collective identity being generated and resurfacing in the emotional regimes and expressions within the team conversations. If they begin to form stable patterns in and around the behaviours associated with these loops this is a sign of strengthening internalization and amplified socialization of the attractor as the team adapts and adopts variations to their initial binary, 'connectedness' norms.

The iterative cycle of reinforcement induced selective perception and group cognition for three of the four, which amplified the 'three against one' binary in their sensemaking and practice. Further reinforcing linked hierarchic relationships at the individual level and in the transition between individual to team learning.

The above case can also be seen to reflect the archetypal systemic loops of the team, especially the recurrence of a 'limits to growth' loop, 'shifting the burden' and 'fixes that backfire' (for example, carrying/assisting/supporting the 'slow' team member) as described by Senge (1990). These loops also operated across the micro (individual)/macro (team) boundary in terms of the personal transitions and development.

Cynefin framework and inward versus outward focus

In complexity research, the border between the contexts in the Cynefin model, for example, can become the boundary at the 'edge of chaos' where real innovation and challenges to 'business as usual' *can* occur in the conversational interaction and dynamics between production of goods and services, distribution and exchange. Such change can occur when 'positive' amplification reinforcing the team's Focus, Will and Capability attractor cycles outwards and into change (Kauffman, 1995, pp. 81–86; Cockburn, 2006, 2008).

So, the framework not only tells us how to approach a set of different situations, but the characteristics also explain enough to help us recognize the situation in which we currently reside. You can have great solutions, but if they are applied in the incorrect context, they will be worthless, or worse, harmful. The boundaries of these domains are not fixed however, and situations can cycle back and forth between the domains or else they may exist at the edges or the interfaces between two zones. To paraphrase Stacey, even though we may not have the precision control we have with machines we can exert the type of direction and steer as we do, for example, when horse riding. Such a steer is good enough for the purposes of the trained rider (Stacey, 2001).

There can be a number of ways in which a border is established, even in open social systems. The border in a social system is clearly not physical, as in a cell, but instead serves a logical or functional purpose (Zeleny, 1996). Thus, for example, the members of a family are determined by their relationship to one another, a company or a team is an entity even if it is dispersed around the globe or entirely virtual, and, neither a doctor nor a sales team leaves the system of the hospital or company as long as they are connected with a beeper. The use of technology can allow for an extension to any communications network although that aspect is not directly relevant to this project.

The idea of the border can be used to clarify that any element which is directly needed to achieve a certain goal is inside the team network. Any element that is able to influence an actor but is not inside the team network belongs to the environment. The team network itself maintains the separation and connection between the two, which occurs at the border. It is this feature of being both simultaneously 'open' and 'closed' which is the foundational paradox of social networks and which links the two.

'Yet Snowden and Weick's models direct us toward developing enough trust that we can empower people to participate in local complex conditions, including the right to respond instantly. If complex change can begin with small, local forces, then having the ears and eyes of observers acting on these forces follows as a strategy. The paradox of "letting go" and remaining involved is one of the hardest complexity responses for a manager to learn' (Browning and Boudès, 2005).

References

Barsade, S.G., 2003. The ripple effect: Emotional contagion and its effect on group behavior. *Administrative Science Quarterly*, 47, pp. 644–675.

Bartel, C.A. and Saavedra, R., 2000. The collective construction of workgroup moods. *Administrative Science Quarterly* 45, pp. 197–231.

Blackburn, S. 2003. Portrait – Richard Rorty, in *Prospect,* pp. 58–64, April.

Brookfield, S., 1983. *Adult Learners, Adult Education and the Community*. Milton Keynes, UK: Open University Press.

Browning, L. and Boudès, T., 2005. The use of narrative to understand and respond to complexity: A comparative analysis of the Cynefin and Weickian models. *Emergency, Complexity and Organization* 7(3–4), p. 38.

Buckley, W., 1968/1973. Society as a complex adaptive system. In G. Salaman, and K.Thompson, eds, 1973. *People and Organisations*. London, UK: Longman.

Cavaye, J.M., 2004. *Performance Measures Framework Implementation and Customisation Project. Final Report.* Melbourne, Australia: Department of Education and Training, Victorian Government, Adult Community and Further Education Division.

Ciborra, C.U. and Lanzara, G.F., 1994. Formative contexts and information technology: Understanding the dynamics of innovation in organizations. *Accounting, Management & Information Technology* 4(2), pp. 61–86.

Cockburn, T.S., 2005. Communities of Commitment: Leadership, Learning Spirals, Teamwork and Emotional Regimes on an MBA, 1997–1999 (available from library of the University of Wales, Cardiff, UK). Unpublished doctoral thesis.

Cockburn, T., 2006. A Complexity Based Typology of Emotional Regimes in Teams. ITPNZ Conference – Research that Counts. Napier, New Zealand, 28–29 September.

Cockburn, T., 2007. Emotionally Sustainable Business and Communities of Commitment. 6th International Conference on Corporate Social Responsibility, Kuala Lumpur, Malaysia, 11–14 June.

Cockburn, T., 2008. The Emotional Landscape of Action Learning MBA Teams. International Action Learning Conference: Action Learning: Practices, Problems & Prospects, Henley Management College, UK, 17–19 March.

Cockburn, T. and Lewis, T., 1999. Images of success: Tacit knowledge collectivized in work-teams. In Kantarlis, D. ed. Business & Economics Society International Conference, *Anthology of Selected Papers*, pp. 224–237.

Cook, S.D.N. and Brown, J.S., 2002. Bridging epistemologies: The generative dance between organisational knowledge and organisational knowing. In Little, S., Quintas, P. and Ray, T. eds, 2002. *Managing Knowledge*. Thousand Oaks, CA: Sage.

Edmondson, A., 2012. *Teaming: How Organizations Learn, Innovate, and Compete in the Knowledge Economy*. San Francisco, CA: Wiley.

Fineman, S., 1996. Emotion and organizing. In Clegg, S.R. and Hardy, C. eds, 1999. *Studying Organizations*. London, UK: Sage.

Giddens, A., 1991. *Self, Identity and Modernity*. London, UK: Polity.

Guarana, C.L. and Hernandez, M., 2015. Building sense out of situational complexity: The role of ambivalence in creating functional leadership processes. *Organizational Psychology Review* 5(1), pp. 50–73.

Hazy, J.K., Goldstein, J.A. and Lichtenstein, B.B. (Eds) 2007. *Complex Systems Leadership Theory New Perspectives from Complexity Science on Social and Organizational Effectiveness*. Mansfield, MA: ISCE Publishing.

Kakihara, M., Soerensen, C. and Wiberg, M., 2002. Fluid interaction in mobile work practice and usually employing devices with RTC. *Proceedings of the First Global Roundtable*, Tokyo, Japan, May 29–30, pp. 1–15.

Kauffman, S., 1995. *At Home in the Universe*. Oxford, UK: Oxford University Press.

Luhmann, N., 1986. The autopoiesis of social systems. In Geyer, F. and van de Zouwen, J. eds, 1986. *Sociocybernetic Paradoxes: Observation, Control and Evolution of Self-steering Systems*. London, UK: Sage.

Lupton, D., 1998. *The Emotional Self*. London, UK: Sage.

Moreland, R.L., Argote, L. and Krishnam, R., 1996. Socially shared cognition at work: Transactive memory and group performance. In Nye, J. and Brouwer, A. eds. *What's Social about Social Cognition? Research on Socially Shared Cognition in Small Groups*. Newbury Park, CA: Sage.

Nonaka, I., 1994. A dynamic theory of organisational knowledge creation. *Organization Science* 5(1), pp. 14–37.

Nonaka, I., 1995. The knowledge-creating company. In Theseus Institute, Sophia Antipolis. Conference on The Emergent Corporation, Nice, France, June 7–10.

Oakes, P., Haslam, S.A. and Turner, J.C., 1998. The role of prototypicality in group influence and cohesion: Contextual variation in the graded structure of social categories. In Worchel, S., Morales, F., Paez, D. and Deschamps, J-C., 1998. *Social Identity*. London, UK: Sage.

Pask, G., 1976. Conversation theory: Applications in education and epistemology. Cited in Scott, B. 2001. Conversation theory: A constructivist, dialogical approach to educational technology. *Cybernetics & Human Knowing* 8 (4), pp. 25–46.

Pask, G., 1980. Developments in conversation theory – Part 1. *International Journal of Man-Machine Studies* 13, pp. 357–411.

Polanyi, M. 1967. *The Tacit Dimension*. Garden City, NY: Anchor Books.

Rimé, B., 2009. Emotion elicits the social sharing of emotion, *Emotion Review* 1(1), pp. 60–85.

Schön, D., 1995. The new scholarship requires a new epistemology. *Change* 27(34), pp. 27–34.

Scott, B., 2001. Conversation theory: A constructivist, dialogical approach to educational technology. *Cybernetics & Human Knowing* 8(4), pp. 25–46.

Senge, P.M., 1990. *The Fifth Discipline: The Art and Practice of the Learning Organization*. New York, NY: Doubleday Currency.

Smith, P.A.C. and Cockburn, T., 2013. *Dynamic Leadership Models for Global Business: Enhancing Digitally Connected Environments*. Hershey, PA: IGI Global.

Smith, E.R. and Mackie, D.M., 1995. *Social Psychology*. New York, NY: Worth Publishers.

Spataro, S.E and Anderson, C., 2002. *Values That Shape Hierarchies: Group Culture and Individuals' Status in Organizations*, Yale University Working Paper OB series, Working Paper #5, Available at: <http://ssrn.com/abstract_id=323663> [Accessed 12, March, 2015].

Spender, J-C., 1998. The dynamics of individual and organisational knowledge. In Eden, C. and Spender, J-C. eds. 1998. *Managerial and Organisational Cognition*. London, UK: Sage.

Stacey, R.D., 2001. *Complex Responsive Processes In Organizations*. London, UK: Routledge.

Stroh, U. and Jaatinen, M., 2000. New approaches to communication management for transformation and change in organizations. 7th International Public Relations Research Symposium, Bled, Slovenia, 7–8 July.

Tight, M., ed., 1983. *Adult Learning and Education*. Milton Keynes: Open University/ Croom Helm.

Valentine, M.A. and Edmondson, A.C., 2014. *Team Scaffolds: How Meso-Level Structures Support Role-based Coordination in Temporary Groups*, Harvard Business School Working Paper 12–062.

Weick, K.E. and Roberts, K.H., 1993. Collective mind in organization: Heedful interrelating on flight decks. *Administrative Science Quarterly* 38, pp. 357–381. In Eden, C. and Spender, J-C. eds. 1998. *Managerial and Organisational Cognition*. London, UK: Sage.

Winograd, T., 1987. A language/action perspective on the design of cooperative work. *Human-Computer Interaction* 3(1), pp. 3–30. Available at: http://www.

hci.stanford.edu/~winograd/papers/language-action.html [Accessed 26 June 2002].

Woolcock, M., 1999. Social capital: The state of the notion. In Multidisciplinary Seminar on Social Capital: Global and Local Perspectives, 15 April, Helsinki, Finland.

Worchel, S., Iuzzini, J., Coutant, D. and Ivaldi, M., 2000. A multidimensional model of identity: Relating individual and group identities to intergroup behaviour. In Capozza, D. and Brown, R. eds. *Social Identity Processes*. London, UK: Sage.

Worchel, S., Morales, F., Paez, D. and Deschamps, J-C., 1998. *Social Identity*. London, UK: Sage.

Zeleny, M., 1996. The social nature of autopoietic systems. In Khalil. E.L. and Boulding, K. eds, 1996. *Evolution, Complexity and Order*. London, UK: Routledge, pp. 122–145.

Chapter 6
Team members' insights

Overview

Emergence team members must understand from the time they have been chosen that essentially all the teamwork and action learning related work is their responsibility; the team leader, as noted in Chapter 3, largely functions as an adviser (as explained in Chapter 4). The required emergence team member insights described in this chapter flow naturally from this division of responsibilities and activities, and the definition of emergence provided in Chapter 1, plus the implications of the action learning and multi-ontological sense-making approach that are also described in Chapter 1. The need for 'order' (to satisfy the multi-ontological sense-making approach) is provided for the team from the sponsor's written guidelines, plus the later sponsor and team leader dialogue and the EMCEE role, and finally through the dialogue with the team members. Team members must therefore understand what dialogue involves and have the skills to engage in it with other people, including fellow team members. This satisfies the need for order, although un-order demands that team members understand and possess the skills necessary to undertake action learning (Wikipedia, 2015), plus sense-making, dialogue, critical reflectivity and interviewing skills. These capabilities help ensure that the team's results will be emergent.

Although this chapter presents information of particular relevance to emergence team members, the team performance is a systemic effort, where the perfection of individual elements is not as important as understanding and optimizing the interaction between the elements. In other words, the emergence team members should read the whole of this book, and through their learning operationalize its recommendations as seamlessly as possible. The same proviso to 'read the whole book' applies to the team leader, the team sponsor, and all other involved and interested personal.

Potential team member problems

The members of emergence teams are typically highly experienced and often experts in their own disciplines. Conflicts among their ideas, opinions, preferences, theories and team perspectives are almost inevitable, especially as each expert often does not perceive the whole problem that the team is tasked with, but rather sees those aspects that are familiar to them. In addition, highly experienced individuals will tend to emphasize the importance of their own particular expertise, and will often reach biased conclusions. Although the team leader will likely be sensitive to these issues, and will attempt to help resolve them, team members themselves must take responsibility for ensuring effective and equitable team decision making. Whether balanced and effective decisions are achieved depends on a constructive approach that each team member must adopt. Such an approach demands that all information be accurately communicated between team members, and that there is a supportive climate where all team members feel safe to challenge each other's ideas. An important skill for each team member to develop is to be able to disagree with other team members, while still confirming the other person's competency. Another important skill is perspective taking; this is involved when personal or impersonal information is exchanged between individuals. In such circumstances it is helpful to paraphrase the information exchanged. This helps to communicate a desire to understand, as does making a deliberate attempt during team sessions to frequently seek out and understand differences among members' ideas and so on.

There are other subtle problems (Johansen et al., 1991) that can beset team members that may not be readily detected and corrected by the team leader, but rather individual team members must guard against. The emergence team will often be under severe time constraints. In this atmosphere, team members may start to prematurely reach conclusions because they feel there is insufficient time to weigh alternatives appropriately. In addition, team members who operate in a slower and more pensive style may find their ideas marginalized. In either case, the team may adopt a wrong path. Another subtle problem occurs when team members find that normal organizational channels are too constraining, and they find ways to bypass organizational road blocks. When team members regularly bypass corporate procedures they may end up alienating themselves from other organizational workers and achieving non-collaborative reputations that may prevent coordinated efforts in the future. Another subtle problem is related to the loyalty that is generated during team operation. Immediate feedback and a strong sense of belonging are engendered in an emergence team. Such personal involvement may conflict with, but must not be allowed to override, personal family commitments or other organizational relationships.

All the skills or problems noted above (except interviewing) are best developed by team members in group (team) practice sessions under the guidance of the team leader acting as a facilitator, coach or adviser. Interviewing on the other hand is normally undertaken in one-on-one sessions involving the interviewer and the interviewee, where facilitation or coaching during the event are not feasible. In our experience 'play-acting' interviewing between team members does not mimic the interpersonal tensions of a real interview and is time that could be better spent on other skills. Interviewing skills are best developed through 'learning by doing' in real-life situations. To help a team member prepare to build appropriate interviewing skills, a longer paragraph describing interviewing has been included later in this chapter.

Action learning processes

Action learning has been highlighted a number of times in earlier chapters. Action learning is a process that has proven capable of solving complex practical problems (Smith and Day, 2000), and is based on a cycle of taking action and reflecting on the results. Waddill and Marquardt (2003) and Waddill (2004) explain that the power of the action learning process is derived from its theoretical underpinnings, and in particular on the strong link between the action learning process and adult learning theory.

The normal face-to-face action learning process typically involves a group (a 'Set') of six people who meet together for a period of time (usually some part of a day initially) over a period of weeks or months, where one person who has a problem very clearly explains their problem to the other members of the Set and then outlines action(s) the problem-holder plans to implement to resolve the problem. The whole Set then helps the problem-holder explore his/her assumptions and reasoning for the action proposed. In so doing, the whole Set is involved in critical reflection and dialogue to help the problem-holder decide on the appropriate action to be taken. It is fundamental to action learning that action is actually taken and not just proposed. After the chosen action(s) have actually been implemented, the Set follows up in a step-wise cyclic manner (see Figure 4.2, Chapter 4). However, it is not unusual for a whole team to be responsible for the problem and seeking a solution (as is the typical case for an emergence team) in the same step-wise cyclic manner indicated in Figure 4.2, Chapter 4. This team approach does place extra constraints on the action learning process, since at the various stages of the step-wise cycle, instead of having five individuals assisting one individual reflect on results, all the participants must help one another. It has been pointed out in the literature that there is an ongoing challenge in action learning when whole teams are involved since there is often reluctance to take the time necessary to adequately reflect on the results of the proposed action, and thus the process does not involve adequate critical reflection to capture the learning that should result. Consequently, in such situations, emphasis is placed on the critical importance of having an action learning coach or adviser. Wellins et al. (1991) have noted that self-managing teams seldom take the time to reflect on what they are doing or make efforts to identify key lessons learned from the process. As a consequence, team members employ assumptions, mental models and beliefs about methods or processes that are seldom openly challenged, much less tested. In emergence teams, the team leader is expected to play the role of action learning adviser or facilitator; this is a good choice because the team leader is aware of the balance that must be struck between a certain amount of order and disorder, and ensures that emergence happens.

Performance learning

The problem, on which the team works is often very complex, and some simplification or structure within the action learning process is helpful; this simplification may be readily accomplished by considering the problem as a performance problem (Smith, 1997). This author names this approach 'Performance Learning'. Figure 4.1 in Chapter 4 displays a dynamic performance model where performance level is a function of Focus, Will and Capability. In Chapter 4 the model is used to address a team leader's role, but the model is generic and we recommend adopting it to address the problem with which the team has been tasked. When this substitution has been accepted, Figure 4.2 in Chapter 4 relates to the 'probe, since and respond' steps in the Cynefin framework. In this case an enabler would be the response that the team believes might help mitigate the problem. The 'think about results' stage in the model will demand that team members possess a number of skills: learning, sensemaking, critical reflectivity and dialogue. These skills form a team community system where command of any one skill is dependent on an individual team member's aptitude in the other skills and on the aptitude of other team members. The team members should note that action learning is frequently practised based strictly according to the process described by its originator Professor Reg Revans (Revans, 2011). This approach is overly 'scientific' and makes no acknowledgment of 'emotional' concerns or pressures that may be present in the human dimensions of the problem. Given that the performance model noted above (Figure 4.1 in Chapter 4) includes a field entitled 'Will', and that it is not logical to ignore emotional elements present in the problem space, we recommend that a form of action learning practised by Roger Gaunt (1991) be utilized. The Gaunt approach is well accepted and widely practised in the UK, and it does include opportunities for appropriate emotional analysis and the process has been described by McLaughlin (1988).

Definition of other important team member skills

'Learning' in this context demands open sharing of knowledge and ideas among all team members, which is clearly, for example, strongly related to skill in dialogue and reflection.

'Sensemaking' is the process by which team members in the 'think about results' stage attach meaning to the results of their 'probe' experience. This is a collaborative process of creating shared awareness and understanding out of team members' different view points and varied interests. 'Critical reflectivity' may be defined as 'the bringing of one's assumptions, premises, criteria, and schemata into consciousness and vigorously critiquing them' (Mezirow, 1981, p. 25). Marsick and Watkins (1990, p. 29) assert that, 'Critical reflectivity is distinguished from a simpler level of reflection in which people think back over what worked or did not work, try to identify observable sources of error in cause-effect relationships, or simply let their attention wander back over an event.'

In 'dialogue', during the 'think about results' stage, the team explores from many points of view, the complex difficult issues related to the results of their 'probe' experience; they do this whilst shelving their assumptions *but* still communicating these assumptions freely. This results in a free exploration that surfaces the full depth of people's experiences and thoughts, and yet can move beyond their personal views so that they may achieve consensus. These assumptions would otherwise cause team members to advance views skewed typically by non-relevant criteria with no hope of reaching consensus.

Much of team members' efforts will be spent in capturing organizational knowledge and experience related to the problem with which the team has been tasked. This knowledge and experience resides in the informal stories that team members encourage organizational members to recount during interviews. These stories are documented such that whole-team examination and sensemaking may be carried out on each documented story, to provide (a) the estimated status of Focus (F), Will (W) and Capability (C) with respect to the problem with which the team has been tasked; and (b) identification of the Cynefin element to which the problem appears to belong.

Deciphering organizational stories

Storytelling is the art of weaving and constructing a product of intimate knowledge. It is a delicate process that can easily break down (Gabriel, 2000). Good storytellers command power and esteem, and their stories can explain, entertain, inspire, educate and convince. Such stories can open valuable windows into the emotional, political and symbolic lives of organizations, and are therefore valuable and cannot be mass produced.

Most such stories are multi-authored and they offer a powerful instrument for carrying out research (Gabriel, 2000). This author further claims that organizational storytelling is an organizational sense-making process; the truth of the story lies not in the facts but in the meaning. According to Gabriel (2000, p. 19), Boje (1991, p. 106) states that organizational storytelling is the institutional memory system of the organization. Gabriel (2000) further asserts that stories describe organizational culture and change in uniquely illuminating ways and are valuable *but precarious* artefacts, since storytelling continuously recreates the past according to the present, and interpretations become stories in their own right. Emergence team members should treat the stories they gather through their interviews as clues to the truth about the organization and the nature of the problem with which the team has been tasked; team members must try to elucidate the facts of the case by asking according to Gabriel (2000, p. 32) questions such as 'When?' 'Where?' and 'How?' Team members should note that these are very similar to the questions related to Focus which are 'Who, What, Where, When, How and Why?'

Team members need to be aware that not all narratives they hear in their interviews are stories – some are factual descriptive accounts of events that need to be identified as such. However, team members should also note that each story invites repetition and further embellishment but it does not invite factual verification. By collecting stories and comparing different accounts, organizational realities can be pictured and linked to organizational members' experiences. The approach of emergence team members should be largely interpretive, seeking to unmask the hidden symbolism, treating the stories as storage boxes of meaning; for example stories may embody theories, rules of thumb, opinions, metaphors, scenarios, arguments and explanations, to name a just a few inclusions (Gabriel, 1999).

Interpreting stories to assess focus, capability and will

The first step is to document the story as narrated by the interviewee. The interviewer, as appropriate, might then pose some of the Focus-related questions listed above. The key issue here is to assess the degree of vagueness of the answers to these questions. Other questions could then be posed to assess the organizational skills and wherewithal available for the organization to try to actualize the Focus indicated by the above questions. Related emotional attitudes could then be assessed by asking questions such as 'How did everybody feel about their chances of successfully solving that problem?' and 'Was there a "we can do this" feeling among the personnel involved?' We do not recommend exploring for metaphors or scenarios with the interviewee; the meanings embodied in the story are best teased out in a later session involving team members.

The fact that an organization has one or more serious performance problems necessitating the formation of an emergence team is a strong indicator that one of the organizational performance drivers (F, W or C) is underdeveloped or absent completely. Unfortunately, as Smith and McLaughlin (2003) assert: the reasons why organizations do not have balanced well-targeted (F, C, W) performance drivers are not logical. These authors explain that typically tacit feeling-laden concerns are involved but are ignored, since most organizations operate under a façade of rationality, even though Will involves irrational issues. As a result, organizations often perceive Will as a negative driver that is related to the expressive arenas of life rather than to the instrumental goal-orientation that drives organizations. Smith and McLaughlin (2003) quote Egan (1973, p. 61): 'Emotional repression in organizations is undoubtedly still a far greater problem than emotional overindulgence.' Smith and McLaughlin (2003) claim that, 'Thirty years later this statement is as true as ever; much of Western society still equates emotional maturity with the control or repression of feelings, continuing to use the word 'emotional' in a belittling sense.' The fields of Capability and Focus are easier for organizations to address, since they involve the production of tangible 'evidence' such as action plans, reports and the like.

Figure 6.1 indicates the Cynefin framework environments that may be inferred from varying combinations of F, W and C ascertained from questions posed to interviewees during interview sessions or through questions explored in team analysis of stories collected. These relationships should only be considered as guidelines, but experience has shown that these drivers may be defined relatively accurately and easily, and often will indicate the nature of the problem space in the Cynefin environment. The F, W, C performance framework has the benefit of conceptual simplicity and elegance and has been found extremely useful as a tool for stimulating discussion of issues related to radical change. Although we do not recommend exploring this performance framework directly in story-gathering interviews, its ability to promote dialogue will be very helpful during team analysis of stories.

Drew and Smith (1995) advance the notion of Change Proofing based on the levels of F, W and C evident in an organization, and explain that Change Proofing is not a means of resisting or avoiding change, but bestows on the organization

CONTEXT	PERFORMANCE DRIVER DEFINITION		
	Focus	**Capability**	**Will**
SIMPLE	WELL DEFINED BUT MAYBE NOT FULFILLED	WELL DEFINED BUT MAYBE NOT FULFILLED	MODERATE OR STRONG
COMPLICATED	LACKS DETAIL	LACKS DETAIL	WEAK DUE TO UNCERTAINTY
COMPLEX	VERY POOR	VERY POOR	NONE OR MISDIRECRED: DUE TO UNCERTAINTY
CHAOTIC	NONE: DUE TO UNCERTAINTY	NONE: DUE TO UNCERTAINTY	NONE: DUE TO UNCERTAINTY
DISORDER	NONE: DUE TO UNCERTAINTY	NONE: DUE TO UNCERTAINTY	NONE: DUE TO UNCERTAINTY

Figure 6.1 Relationships between Cynefin contexts and performance drivers

the ability to cope with significant complex change when it eventuates. Change Proofing is a process for becoming more flexible and responsive, by developing the ability to recognize and respond to early signals of complex change or unanticipated opportunities. Drew and Smith (1995) suggest that the level of Change Proofing (the levels of F, W and C) may be judged from the responses to a questionnaire submitted to the organization's employees or through employee stories.

'Focus' signifies a clear sense of direction and vision. It arises from strategic thinking, knowledge and understanding of the organization's key decision making groups and it may be judged from statements (or sentiments) roughly expressed in an interview as:

1. we all know how our company is overcoming competitive challenges;

2. the organization's future goals are clear to all employees;

3. everyone around here knows the best way to get their work done;

4. employees know that their contribution are valued;

5. we have access to all the information we need to do our jobs;

6. employees and managers have a clear picture of the firm's strategy.

'Capability' signifies having the skills, budgets, infrastructure and so on to implement the performance defined in Focus, and may be judged from statements (or sentiments) roughly expressed in an interview as:

1. we are well trained to fulfil our roles;

2. resources are available when required;

3. team work around here is excellent;

4. we possess core competences that distinguish our firm from the competition;

5. our competitors regularly benchmark our firm's products and services;

6. the firm has a reputation for satisfying, and going beyond, customer expectations.

'Will' signifies individual and collective intent to implement the performance defined in Focus, and may be judged from statements (or sentiments) roughly expressed in an interview as:

1. there is a high level of self-confidence in my team;

2. the work we do here is very meaningful to me;

3. I have a strong sense of belonging to this organization;

4. I willingly put in extra effort when we get behind in our work;

5. the company and I have substantially the same values;

6. I trust this organization has my interests at heart.

The emotional issues highlighted by Smith and McLaughlin (2003), and by Smith and Cockburn in Chapter 5 of this book, highlight further concerns to which emergence team members should be sensitive as they seek to unravel the stories they have collected through their interviews. Gabriel (1999, p. 217) asserts that it is not possible to bring to life every emotional nuance present in a story since the story may evoke different emotions in different individuals, and the narrator himself, or herself, may have ambiguous or confused feelings about his or her material. Work situations arouse very strong and mixed feelings in employees (Menzies Lyth, 1988) and in recounting stories these feelings may persuade individuals to project a very unrealistic picture of their organization's activities. Gabriel alludes to a story that on telling resulted in mirth and amusement among the listeners, although the actual events that were the subject of the story at the time generated serious concerns. Sometimes, members of an organization call a truce to an interpersonal conflict or disagreement and mimic roles drawn from family life, that provide them with models for anxiety containment; in this way they avoid addressing the dysfunction (Gabriel, 1999). However the price they pay for such a truce is the creation of a taboo subject that may not be spoken of, even in stories, which then perpetuates the disagreement. Hirschhorn (1988) claims that successful organizations in the future will need members who confront and work through dysfunctions rather than members who identify scapegoats to victimize; this victimization typically involves recounting 'funny' demeaning stories that may indicate an overdeveloped 'Will'.

Bureaucratic organizations contain features which act as systematic generators of anxiety. Such organizations are typically hierarchical and although this helps to define responsibilities it also results in ambiguities that are compounded by the impersonality and distance between individuals across organizational boundaries. The empty spaces between subordinates and supervisors become filled with fantasies which then set off anxieties, and individuals then adopt defensive tactics such that they 'cover their butts' at all times. Blaming, victimizing and scapegoating are all derived from this bureaucracy and become entrenched in the emotional life of the organization (Gabriel, 1999). Blame travels up and down hierarchies whereby superiors blame subordinates for carrying out the wrong actions, and subordinates blame superiors for improper direction or planning. Such continued levels of anxiety generate alarmist gossip and horror stories of injustice and humiliation. Such stories are then embellished and passed on, and become established 'truths' in company folklore. These fantasies then shape the organization's work world and defeat efforts at organizational enlightenment.

Emergence team members must be vigilant for signs of the above problems in their interpretation of stories that they collect through their interviews. Team members must also watch for indications that senior members of the organization have fixed mental models and a resistance to learning, since these traits will result in demotivated employees (Smith and Saint-Onge, 1996). Team members must also bear in mind that regardless of the F or C value *or* the environment identified, if there is no Will to implement plans, there will be no action, and whether the problem to be addressed is complex or complicated is of little importance since the organization is doomed.

Interviewing

Interviewing is one of the distinctive skills that emergence team members must master. As the following paragraphs will show, interviewing takes a great deal of skill if it is to produce significant kinds of information that shed light on the problem. Team members must get into people's heads to find out what hasn't been written down. This must be accomplished without 'official' leverage. Interviewing under these circumstances depends crucially on the interviewer's knowledge of the problem situation. This knowledge helps to generate mutual respect in the interview. This respect also depends to a large extent on the interviewer's interpersonal skills. In this regard, it will help if the interviewer can generate a sense of the importance of the interview in solving the overall problem. The interviewer should demonstrate intense curiosity; for example, by hanging on to, and exploring the implications of, the interviewee's every word. This develops energy which enables both participants to gain greater insight than either could have gained alone.

As indicated above, interviews will typically involve encouraging the interviewee to tell their story, and an interview should not be treated as a conversation, or a simple storytelling session, even though the interviewer may want the person being interviewed to believe that this is the case! This is because a conversation or story often jumps from one topic to another, following paths that have resulted from topics that have been mentioned moments before; all of this will be difficult for the interviewer to sort out. The interviewer also needs to be aware that interviewees invariably avoid recounting uncomfortable events. A good interview, on the other hand, is carefully structured and delivered to facilitate the logical, largely one-way, transfer of information/story from source to interviewer. Although the interviewer typically controls the topics, the interviewee controls the information. For this to happen successfully the interview must be based on research and preparation by the interviewer, but also to some extent will depend upon the experience of the interviewer. The team leader may need to assess the interviewing experience of team members and assign the most experienced individual to collect a particularly important story.

The interviewer must first understand the topic plus as much as possible about the interviewee. The content of the questions to be asked is determined by the nature of the problem, plus how the interviewee responds and what the interviewer intends to find out. Questions may be divided into 'personal', 'impersonal' and 'abstract', and also subcategorized into 'hot', 'neutral' and 'cool' according to the interviewee's degree of emotional involvement. 'Hot' questions probe the interviewee's personal *experience*; 'neutral' questions explore the interviewee's arms-length *knowledge* of matters in which they are or were, not involved directly; and 'cool' questions deal with concepts and principles with little or no emotional relevance. The list of questions should have been prepared by the interviewer before the interview, and these questions should be kept simple. For example, interviewers should avoid:

- long-winded questions;

- questions that betray the interviewer's own opinions;

- multiple questions that leave the interviewee to choose which question to answer;

- questions that imply blame;

- closed-ended questions.

Critical interviews are best carried out face-to-face rather than by telephone or other distant means.

Clearly, team members cannot expect to transform themselves overnight into confident poised knowledgeable interviewers. However, team members should concentrate on first developing knowledge, then demeanour and then finally the technique. Appearing bored or hostile or fearful will certainly affect the interview negatively. Very often in the first few minutes of an interview an exchange will take place which will significantly impact the tone of the interview for better or for worse. To influence this exchange positively the interviewer must develop an appropriate demeanour, for example not appearing hesitant or apologetic, nor too forceful or demanding, but rather confident and relaxed.

Good interviewers master the art of listening and concentrate solely on the interviewee ignoring any other distractions. A good interview is like a story with a beginning that then unfolds according to the interviewer's plan. Most interviewees will be nervous, and the interviewer should do their best to set the interviewee at ease. The interview should be structured with the factual questions first – then once this is done, it is time to tackle the contentious or personal questions. The interviewer may use silence judiciously during the interview. The interviewer finally signals that the interview is over and might then ask if the interviewee would like to address anything that has not already been covered.

Organizing and writing the story-based narrative

When the research phase is over, its time to begin organizing and writing the story that has been elicited or that the information has portrayed. It is essential that the interviewer be organized right from the beginning of the investigative phase, keeping a chronological database listing for example:

- the interview date;

- the interviewees' name;

- the interviewers' name;

- the principal story topic (brief);

- any associated documentation;

- any important facts or questions that have come to mind during the investigative phase;

- a transcription of the interview;

- details of any incidents that have been, or could be substantiated by a reliable secondary source.

References

Boje, D.M., 1991. The storytelling organization: A study of story performance in an office-supply firm. *Administrative Science Quarterly* 36, pp. 106–126.

Drew, S.A.W. and Smith, P.A.C., (1995).The learning organization: 'Change proofing' and strategy. *The Learning Organization* 2(1), pp. 4–14.

Egan, G., 1973. *Face To Face*. Monterey, CA: Brooks/Cole.

Gabriel, Y. 1999. *Organizations in Depth*. London, UK: Sage.

Gabriel, Y. 2000. *Storytelling in Organizations: Facts, fictions, and fantasies.* Oxford, UK: Oxford University Press.

Gaunt, R. 1991. *Personal and Group Development for Managers: An integrated approach through action learning*. Harlow, UK: Longmans.

Hirschhorn, L. 1988. *The Workplace Within*. Cambridge, MA: MIT Press.

Johansen, R., Sibbet, D., Benson, S., Martin, A., Mittman, R. and Saffo, P., 1991. *Leading Business Teams*. Reading, MA: Addison-Wesley.

Mclaughlin, M., 1988. Action learning. *Counselling at work* Autumn, pp. 9–10. Available at: <www.mclaughlinassociates.co.uk> [Accessed 23 March 2015].

Marsick, V.J. and Watkins, K.E., 1990. *Informal and Incidental Learning in the Workplace*. London, UK: Routledge.

Menzies Lyth, I., 1988. The Functioning of Social Systems as a Defence against Anxiety. In *Containing Anxiety in Institutions*. London: Free Associations.

Mezirow, J.D., 1981. A critical theory of adults learning and education. *Administrative Science Quarterly* 32(1), pp. 3–27.

Revans, R.W. 2011. *ABC's of Action Learning*. Burlington, VT: Gower.

Smith, P.A.C. 1997. Performance learning. *Management Decision* 35(10), pp. 721–730.

Smith, P.A.C. and Cockburn, T., 2016. *Developing and Leading Emergence Teams*. Farnham, UK: IGI Global.

Smith, P.A.C. and Day, A., 2000. Strategic planning as action learning. *Organisations & People* 7(1), p. 2000.

Smith, P.A.C. and McLaughlin, M. 2003. Succeeding with knowledge management: Getting the people-factors right. Paper presented at 6th World Congress on Intellectual Capital & Innovation, January 15–17 2003, McMaster University, Hamilton, Canada.

Smith, P.A.C. and Saint-Onge, H., 1996. The evolutionary organization: Avoiding a Titanic fate. *The Learning Organization* 3(4), pp. 4–21.

Waddill, D., 2004. *Action E-Learning: The Impact of Action Learning on the Effectiveness of a Management-level Web-based Instruction Course*. Ann Arbor, MI: UMI.

Waddill, D.D. and Marquardt, M., 2003. Adult learning orientations and action learning. *Human Resource Development Review* 2(4), pp. 406–429.

Weick, K.E., 1995. *Sensemaking in Organizations*. Thousand Oaks, CA: Sage.

Wellins, R.S., Byham, W.C. and Wilson, J.M., 1991. *Empowered Teams: Creating Self-directed Work Teams that Improve Quality, Production, and Participation*. San Francisco, CA: Jossey-Bass.

Wikipedia, Action Learning, 2015. Available at: <http://en.wikipedia.org/wiki/Action_learning> [Accessed 10 February 2015].

Chapter 7
Team intelligence-in-action

Today competition is global and 'world class' technology is increasingly the normal expectation of customers. The strategic management of corporate positioning, market share enhancement and new product development are critical objectives for businesses of all kinds. The key role of identity and brand management in the turbulent e-business world environment requires greater effort at the customer interface, building trust, reliability and confidence. In a period where rapid organizational co-evolution is also occurring there is great potential for anomie in distributed, networked or virtual enterprises. The sustainable management of staff teams for service delivery and successful project completion includes accessing tacit intellectual capital of teams as well as clients.

Although recently criticized for some of its claims, Gibbons et al.'s publication in 1994 indicated that there are two modes of new knowledge production, mode 1 and mode 2 (Hessels and van Lente, 2008). Some still see that work and later research by the authors as still lacking 'a balanced combination of conceptual refinement and empirical testing' (Hessels and van Lente, 2010, p. 69). Gibbons et al. proposed that in many innovative areas, the 'mode 2' form of new knowledge and innovation process tends to dominate. That is, practical applications have raced ahead of complete theoretical exposition of the fields. In other words, the applied elements are the drivers of change and new knowledge development today. That is a process opposed to the traditional academic forms of research, wherein explicitly identified theoretical constructs come first and are used to determine the development of new knowledge before any consideration is given to how the theory is to be applied to practice. Hessels and Lente (2010) do have some cause for their criticisms although it is also true to say, as has been noted in other research (Pfeffer and Fong, 2002; Alutto et al., 2008; Gill and Bhattacherjee, 2009), that few business people read or consider adopting many ideas in the academic business literature today.

Critically, however, Gibbons et al. (1994) and others such as Nonaka and Takeuchi (1995) recognized the importance and the underlying presence of tacit knowledge within organizations, which they identified as a critical component of future organizational learning and development, including the subsequent development of explicit theories. Gibbons et al. (1994) suggested much of the knowledge generated in the international economy is tacit rather than explicit and as we get further into the knowledge era, the major challenge facing most firms will be that of capturing tacit knowledge and thereby linking the internal knowledge management with external opportunities. So, we may ask, how do businesses innovate and differentiate themselves from the rest?

The answer is in terms of their creativity in capturing and applying tacit knowledge to their business. This is expressed in a number of ways: through corporate strategic vision initially but then through the leadership and management of the process of implementation and value creation within the networked business world. So leadership is shown in terms of both processes and products; the creative articulation of the process of symbolic and physical value exchanges within communication networks (Simpson et al., 2005; Cockburn, 2005; Cockburn et al., 2006; Smith and Cockburn, 2013, 2014). The developing knowledge industries of the new economy are especially likely to be differentiated in terms of the innovative business process models, products and service as lead times are often as low as one year for new developments. Previously, the tendency in leadership literature and general business literature has been to regard the creative process as a 'front end only' element. However, it is increasingly apparent that this trend is changing in leading-edge organizations and in the focus of many countries' formal higher education systems (Lewis and Cockburn, 2001a, 2001b; Cockburn, 2005).

The 'consumers' of today extend beyond corporate customers in a number of directions such as the family and community in our view. Specifically, the term 'consumers' in relation to teams and leadership not only includes subordinates but also a range of other stakeholders both inside and outside of the organization. In the dynamically interconnected, 24/7, 'always on' world of today's digital natives and consumers, the line between work lives and personal lives continues to fade into the background. Academics and consultants have also recently recognized that liminality is the norm for many individuals in mobile or temporary positions, for teams and organizations in the new virtual as well as face-to-face workplace and VUCA context with corresponding high on-the-job learning and unlearning allied to emotional resilience expected as a corollary.

To stake a claim in e-business future territory, organizations should be realigning their existing expertise so as to be ready for the time when, as described in Martin's millennium trends discourse, '"Cybereconomy goes main street" with new breeds of online customers, and the "Wired workforce takes over" as virtual work communities leading to new workplace dynamics in an age when

"Open-Book corporations emerge" and boundaries between inside and outside blur or disappear as power shifts to recipients of products, information, services' (Martin, 1999, p. 5). That is already part of the present we inhabit. The challenges for us in this new environment require greater use of 'right hemisphere' abilities and a more systemic understanding and awareness of the dynamics of complexity.

The four levels of systems thinking that teams and leaders must address as a matter of course, according to Senge (19990) are:

- Events that are isolated, apparently random, occurrences with no visible pattern or discernable trends. An example would be where there appears to be some unfortunate, unforeseen 'accidents' that delay the team in meeting its targets.

- Patterns of behaviour that indicate (an apparent) general 'drift'/direction. The patterns may highlight a sense of urgency or of laxity, for instance, but do not suggest answers or any means to make changes to the perceived trends necessarily. For example, the team may notice that time is catching up with them and the project deadline is looming whilst they continue to suffer mishaps or losses of some kind such as absent members, broken tools and so on.

- Systemic structure shows interrelationships between patterns of behaviour. For example, the team may note that because they are trying to make up for absent colleagues and catch up with work to meet fixed/agreed deadlines, they work even harder, taking on more tasks and have to learn new skills or technologies not originally assigned them. This, in turn, increases their susceptibility to illness and stress, causing additional cycles of absences or poor work/output and higher workloads, more late nights as the time passes and other aspects of the environment get more urgent and so on. They might then decide to try to 'work smarter' rather than harder in future.

- Mental models indicate the basic cultural level assumptions (according to Schein there are three levels) but have a meta-level applicability. For example, the team might work smarter but what underlying socialized and internalized values encouraged these kinds of team behaviours in the first place?

In order to practically encourage the process and awaken team members to the need to critically examine their own and others' 'editorial' conversations around their 'team story' and related subtexts in teams' actions or project discussions, a systematic approach must be adopted. That is, we must promote reflection-in-action, that is reflections in real time, upon the ongoing interactive processes of social construction of a team story as it is unfolding. So that type of reflection threads through the tapestry of conversations within teams, between teams, and between teams and the rest of organization or other, external entities.

A team story has been described as the ways that people make sense of, or build coherence from, their fragmented experiences in the context or landscape they are embedded within (Cockburn et al., 2005). We use the term here to capture the sense that the team is trying to 'live the brand', to enact the shared, tacit and explicit values in their practice and everyday actions or behavioural routines as well as the transformational and transitional phases of their work processes.

Thresholds of change

However, emergence teams by definition often stand at the liminal thresholds of imminent surprise and discontinuous change landscapes brimming with implicit promise and threat as well as explicit knowledge and systems. Their considered actions must always aim to invoke collective learning in order to survive and thrive within the quicksilver contexts of their location within the interweave of people, technology and markets in the team's web of relationships. As we remarked elsewhere, as spiders live in the webs they construct, so too teams inhabit and look outwards at the world beyond the webs of relationships they weave. Such webs are not merely techno-social structures to enable them to better engage in business but enable their manner of living and acting and thinking about their environment.

The notion of thresholds of change used here includes the idea of learning thresholds. That is a domain of action where double-loop learning occurs which challenges pre-existing learning and former learning paradigms.

Threshold concepts, discussed in relation to teaching and learning are characteristically defined as follows:

- *Transformative* – occasioning a 'significant shift in the perception of a subject'.

- (Probably) *Irreversible* – 'the change in perspective occasioned by acquisition of a threshold concept is unlikely to be forgotten'.

- *Integrative* – exposing the 'previously hidden interrelatedness of something'.

- (Possibly often) *Bounded* – 'any conceptual space will have terminal frontiers, bordering with thresholds into new conceptual areas'.

- (Potentially) *Troublesome* – that which appears 'counter-intuitive, alien (emanating from another culture or discourse), or incoherent (discrete aspects are unproblematic but there is no organising principle)' (Meyer et al., 2006, pp. 7–9).

The perception of a threshold of change may itself be intuitive or tacit and so we need some means of eliciting and extracting such latent learning and knowledge. We have reviewed and applied a number of models of these processes as they relate to teams in our research. These are discussed briefly below with reference to collective learning, individual and collective transitions, and leadership roles.

Tuckman's (1965) model of team development for instance was discussed in an earlier chapter. Emotions and cognition are noted in Tuckman's model but the behavioural action is fore-grounded. Although they are viewed as being relevant, emotions are treated in a behaviourist-like fashion as lower-order concerns. It is a descriptive rather than analytical model in this respect. No expression of the relationship between these processes and the behaviours at each stage of the team development process is provided. Only the progress through each stage is affected, that is, faster or slower depending on the cognitive-affective interactions. The stages are the same irrespective of the emotions.

Emotions are however very pertinent to the pace and quality of team bonding, development and the anchoring of collective intellectual and social capital in their routine team project behaviours. Emotional maturation processes are thus underpinned by both tacit and explicit sets of norms. We originally used Fineman's (1996) definition of emotional regimes, defined originally as comprising 'the coherent rules governing the complex, emotional "acts and practices" underpinning the teams' shared values, cognitive schemata and enacted scripts'. However, the definition was subsequently amended to, 'The dynamic and responsive relationship processes and coherent rules governing the complex, emotional "acts and practices" underpinning the groups' shared values, schemata and enacted scripts.'

Although we agree that individuals are autonomous agents, this does not preclude interconnections within the team and between the individual and the team as a self-organizing learning vehicle. There is no mention of interconnectedness of the emotional development (of the whole team and of the individual members of the team) by Tuckman. Movement per se is not too well represented by this model although it does draw our attention to discernible transitions in explicit behaviours. These transitions are important in terms of complexity and we have now begun to review them in relation to attractors.

Reflecting the multi-spiral model of tacit knowledge-creation in teams including the transitions in the process of conversion from 'individuals' activity' to collective knowledge in a team occurs from inside out (Cockburn and Lewis, 1999a). However, this 'team-insider' model of knowledge transformation and learning has to be distinguished from the movement of an individual from being a solo learner to being a team learner (Cockburn et al., 2005, 2006). Nonaka's research is not about the 'outsider' or notional 'apprentice' community member becoming an 'insider' or full member as in Wenger's communities of practice model (1998) but, instead, it is about the conversion, transformation and co-creation of knowledge *within* the team and how this may be surfaced explicitly in organizations. That is, the insider's progress through the body of a collective, which transmits learning and reconstitutes the collective anew in a learning-enriched form (Nonaka, 1991, 1994, 1995, 2000; Nonaka and Teece, 2001).

For Nonaka, metaphors cut across people's imaginative perceptions and literal cognitive activities. This model recognizes that symbols are often employed in tacit knowledge and learning. Consequently, the appropriate use of language in the interactions between team members and in the recording and model building thereafter bridges the gap between figurative and logical expression, according to Nonaka:

> *The association of meanings by metaphor is mostly driven by intuition, and involves images. On the other hand, the association of meanings through analogy is more structural/functional and is carried out through rational thinking. As such, metaphors provide much room for free association (discontinuity). Analogy allows the*

> *functional operation of new concepts or systems to be explored by reference to things that are already understood. In this sense, an analogy – that enables us to know the future through the present – assumes an intermediate role in bridging through rational thinking gap between image and logic.*
>
> (Nonaka, 1994, p. 21)

Nonaka's original model has echoes of earlier work such as Senge's (1990) and some even before that, such as Jung's (1981) psychology which linked the unconscious to the conscious experience through the archetypal mental models employed in intuitive judgement as seen in the quotation below.

> *An archetypal content expresses itself, first and foremost, in metaphors. If such a content should speak of the sun and identify with it the lion, the king, the hoard of gold guarded by the dragon, or the power that makes for the life and health of man, it is neither the one thing nor the other, but the unknown third thing that finds more or less adequate expression in all these similes, yet – to the perpetual vexation of the intellect – remains unknown and not to be fitted into a formula.*
>
> ('The Psychology of the Child Archetype', CW 9i: par. 267)

Although referring to individuals, Jung nevertheless recognized their connection to the collective. The team level of being is the equivalent organizational interface of the singular and the plural most manageable for individuals at an explicit, conscious level. In addition, the complex, non-linear dynamics of self-organizing teams can be used, we would argue, as a fractal of the larger, organizational community. Teams exhibit the same systems of attractors and dissipative structures, which complexity theorists propose for corporations and are in line with the concept of fractal development (Cockburn, 2005, 2006). Each individual's process of self-reinvention within the team context may express the psychology of the Jungian archetypes as in the quotation above. However, in a complex responsive process, the achievement of a collective intelligence-in-action is not the result of hierarchy and planning so much as a self-organizing property of a distributed set of intelligences coalescing in the team action and emerging as a collective expression of the integrated 'personality' of the whole.

Thus one method to make the story more 'explicit' is to use 'critical incidents' and Argyris's (in Senge et al., 1994) 'ladder of inference' to illustrate how teams engage in collaborating and learning their team story or what sorts of 'in use' theory and practice is being deployed at any time. By using a range of learning tools and methods discussed below, teams are encouraged to adopt a reflexive approach to their team 'storybuilding' and communication practice. Other methods are adapted from techniques employed for the purposes of exposing alternative ways of framing or interpreting data and stories. Although such methods are not typically accepted in traditional action learning Sets, we recommend their adoption by emergence teams. So we have adopted and suitably adapted tools and techniques such as Bean's (2001) 'decentring' technique, which aims to provide opportunities for students to recognize conflicting perspectives on a topic, and that the truth is something that is socially constructed.

In this context we use the term critical to suggest both critical thinking and to include critical theory. We aim to encourage team members to openly identify, analyse and critique actual or potential hidden tensions, assumptions and meanings within their team processes, thinking and actions (Alvesson and Deetz, 2000). 'Dialogue' enables insights to be challenged and team members may be encouraged to adopt a standpoint on a topic that is different from, and sometimes contradictory to, their own beliefs to simulate the kind of 'competitive collaboration' practices which some Japanese organizations employ according to Nonaka (1995, Nonaka and Teece, 2001).

Intelligence-in-action also involves intuitive artistry

Behaviours in teams are typically focused in three key activity domains. They are about doing the job, that is, directly work-focused, task-related behaviours. They are also about 'maintenance' behaviours to promote team social harmony and in parallel individual behaviours, that is, about peoples' private agendas or ambitions. These three dimensions are:

- the information level;
- the procedural level;
- the emotional level.

Brown et al. (1995) referred to communities of practice using the same tools of the trade differently and cite carpenters and joiners who use identical tools but in different ways. Schön goes beyond the latter reference to the ways that tools are used, extending discussion into the tacit knowledge exhibited by skilled practitioners in respect of how both the tools and the materials being worked also dynamically interact as the work activity proceeds. He is concerned with the consequent adjustments and application of such knowledge by competent practitioners. He is careful to ensure that we are not solely referring to skills but to 'intelligence-in-action' that includes recognition and judgement (Schön, 1994, 1995, 1996).

We argue that the tacit knowledge often referred to is really tacit 'knowing'; adapting Blackler et al.'s (1993/1998) definition, which is that knowledge has been considered a commodity or a noun when it should be viewed as a verb or a process. The key question then is, 'How do people do their knowing?'(Blackler et al., 1998 in Von Krogh et al., 1998, p. 74). There is an immanent or emergent character to it as it evolves and emerges from the context of team formation. Thus, there is also a temporal frame of reference, which is future-directed, and co-intentional whilst nevertheless recognizing the dynamic character of open systems. We visualize an intended future to be enacted but recognize the dynamic complexity and potential surprise elements inherent in social action as well as the opportunities for exploration and development offered by chance events. Therein lies the creative and intuitive artistry and the possibility of 'insight'.

Equally, though, there is an action-orientation of such knowing. It is purposefully geared to doing something. It is an activity system linking cognition and behaviour. We believe that some of the literature neglects the *organizationally*-purposeful activity in favour of the *academically*-purposeful activity of research for theory development. Whilst we recognize this as a potentially critical factor in team development, it is based on the assumption of an individual's identity as fixed and composed mainly of an exclusivity defined in relatively non-permeable, professional boundaries. This is similar to looking for meanings in the stories rather than meaning in the storytelling as Sparrow (1999, p. 181) noted. Even when referring to Gibbons et al.'s (1994) work on multi-discipline groups and tacit learning, Blackler et al. (1998, in Von Krogh et al., 1998, p. 83) do not emphasize enough that the driver is not the academic domain experts but the practical, business-oriented teams seeking practical or commercial applications *before* developing theory rather than the reverse. That is, the so-called 'mode II' forms of knowledge production apply. There is a central issue therefore in how assessment functions on live, real-time, workplace team projects. Namely, how we might develop and evaluate the optimum means to capture/to recycle and/or extend both reflection-in-action and so capture the intelligence-in-action.

Co-creation dilemmas: Intentionality, commitment and tacit knowledge capture

As we have already outlined, there is a movement from passive to active forms of learning in the development of teams as they engage with their project tasks (Cockburn and Lewis, 1999a; Cockburn and Cockburn-Wootten, 2000). The artistry in the process involves judiciously exercising the interpersonal skills of tolerance for learning from 'error' and the willingness to accept alternative perspectives or approaches, which may challenge your own values and beliefs. It means 'boundary scanning' on each project, with each team, and balancing consistency of assessment with uniqueness of the experiences and projects. There is no 'one best way' to do this and staff often fears loss of control. It is important that the 'stories' of the community are not simply rationalizations of behaviour or individuals' powers but reflect double-loop learning of the team. That is, they *constructively* challenge individuals' pre-existing mental models.

The shared experience is, nonetheless, vital to the crystallization of the organizational knowledge network in university education as much as in industry. The dialectical tension between the individual and the corporate is part of the spiral process of moving to a higher Hegelian-type synthesis, according to Nonaka (1994). That synthesis occurs as the teams overcome the lower levels of conflict between member's individuality and the requirement to subordinate the latter to the agreed need for some form of team discipline to achieve their set tasks. Intentionality in purposeful activity is reflected in cognition, knowing and understanding of something, in a social arena. I are not referring to unintended or unintentional efforts either since these are action-oriented project teams. Nonaka (1994) thus connects ontology and epistemology. That is the team's ways of being in the world and their ways of thinking about the world.

However, there is a dilemma in trying to do so using traditional kinds of project assessment processes that are often concerned with assessor-centred outcomes rather than team-centred, developmental outcomes. Traditional project assessment processes, geared to a reductionist paradigm that assumes only one, legitimate, explicit form of knowledge pose dilemmas of rigour and relevance (Cockburn et al., 2005, 2006; Smith and Cockburn, 2013, 2014). How can the relevant tacit knowledge be recognized and assessed using methods which regard such knowledge as invisible, unattainable or illegitimate? Lastly, how can new methods be devised which can attempt to capture the intelligence-in-action as well as reflections-in-action, which necessarily involve some consideration of the mediating impact of perception on cognition and action? Particularly where, as Schön indicates, there is no apparent antecedent reasoning in much of it – it is intuitive, holistic and immediate (Schön, 1995, p. 29). Thus, for example, when we see people we know, we recognize them at once. We do not go through a process of elimination of alternatives as say, a computer, might do. The person is recognized in one go, in a holistic fashion. In traditional assessment, the net effect very often, it seems, is that a simple aggregation of data or bits of information is taken to be equivalent to knowledge and theoretical knowledge is seen as the same as practice (Revans, 1996, p. 75).

There is a second dilemma in the need to 'surface the undiscussables'. The latter is the name for the process of challenging the latent inferences and mental models that are constructed by people about how the world works (Argyris and Schön, 1978; Argyris and Schön, 1996; Argyris, 1986, 1991, 1996). That is, unspoken assumptions are made which orient discussions and reflection on what is observed of processes or of objects uncovered. The 'ladder of inference' technique is one method recommended by Argyris and others (Senge et al., 1994, pp. 239–252). This requires considerable social skills on the part of teams in order to encourage honest expression required of inquiry whilst also balancing that with the awareness of the possibly highly charged emotional dialogue, which can ensue as a result.

The tools and techniques one of the authors have developed previously, such as the 'cast and props', the 'belief box' and the 'walkback' are not hard to use but they allow access and assessment of tacit dimensions (Cockburn and Lewis, 1999b; Cockburn and Cockburn-Wootten, 2000). These techniques also avoid the problems associated with making the story conform to accepted, 'surface-level' or explicit intentions and enabling creative 'branching out' into new directions to probe, explore and/or exploit opportunities as well as reacting to challenges.

The cast and props is a metaphorical technique for capturing the tacit dimensions of developing a shared vision in a team. The walkback is the process of enacting the corporate vision using a form of reverse engineering to review and address issues in their formative assessment of project progress and achievements. The team members carry out the process of constructing the shared vision using the 'cast and props' method. The 'props' may be physical such as equipment or psychological such as attitudes, and the 'cast' are all the parties involved, their roles in the story, which precedes the achievement of the team's shared vision. The 'walkback' takes them through the process of enactment of the story. It is only at the walkback stage that the actual drama is played out for real. During this whole process the individuals and teams go through a number of stages and states in moving from passive to active team learners in real time on action learning projects.

The iterative and evolutionary 'walkback' process serves to materialize the team vision for all as a collaboratively constructed outcome. It also means there are integrated values and beliefs embedded in it which, although possibly multifaceted, are nonetheless compatible with the outcome being achieved by teams as opposed to clusters of individuals. It is the intuitive artistry encapsulated in the discussions and articulations of the latter, which, we believe, need to be captured in project assessments but are often neglected or missed entirely. The value of such creative processes is increasingly apparent to many as globalization proceeds. The model of learning and the tools and techniques we refer to involve the creative and interpretive team process of the assessment and management of a range of resources in real time on a live project. The team's reflections on the latter process, encapsulated in a metaphorical 'cast and props', is used to devise and then enact a corporate vision. The enactment occurs as part of the operationalization of the 'walkback' process (Cockburn and Lewis, 1999a; Cockburn and Cockburn-Wootten, 2000). The above processes are neither one-dimensional nor are they executed in one attempt. The process is iterative. Consequently we require an explicit and critically reflexive '3D' model for team development and to enable enactment of better 3D team working.

Measuring team success

A prototype tool is required for measuring key factors in the development of teams' emotional webs as part of the measurement of their progress and successful embodiment and enactment of the transition from metaphor to metonymy in the project they are engaged upon. It may be periodically applied to an emergence team or to other kinds such as a small to medium enterprise (SME)/start-up, cross-functional team, department or strategic business unit (SBU).

E-WEB METRIC

This tool will assess the following interlinked dimensions:

- project/work commitment;
- trust;
- anxiety;
- leadership style;

- decision making;
- organization of work;
- output quality.

The scale evaluates the perceived ways that project/work commitment is enacted in terms of trust and anxiety is impacted by the other four items on these two key axes of trust (vertical axis) and anxiety (horizontal axis)

The team names in each of the quadrants above reflect characteristics of the teams that inhabit the quadrant. Thus, 'Acephalous' teams lack any core or centre in relation to achieving their project aims and objectives, and have low trust and equally low anxiety about achieving the aims of the group so tend to pair bond with fellow professionals or engage in other non-project-related forms of sociability. On the other side, 'Splits' as the names suggest

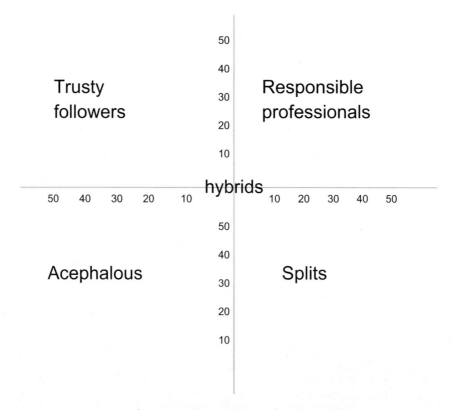

Figure 7.1   Matrix of emotional regimes exhibited in teams

have a tendency to form antagonistic or competitive subgroups or cliques and are suspicious of each other and so may sabotage team aims for clique aims or power reasons. 'Trusty followers' trust the official team 'leader' implicitly and rely on this person for instruction and guidance but are high in project commitment as a result. The 'Responsible professionals' are those with a professional-level approach and high in trust and commitment to team and project. Hybrids are in the centre and reflect a mix with no strong predisposition in terms of trust or project anxiety and commitment (Cockburn, 2005, 2006).

A 3D scale is constructed by taking account of the depth of the 'action dimension' of the team over time on project. The scores on each axis are plotted against the relevant one below and may be linked across to give a web-like, visual showing areas for attention/enhancement/rebalancing and so on. This might be redone any number of times to reveal individual leader/units'/teams' patterns of change over time – again in a web-like shape – leading to a 'why?' from the inverted 'Y'. May be colour-coded for all separate iterations and a combined team version compiled to show strengths/weaknesses across leadership or parts of team or other functional groups/ teams Having the metrics allows a strategic review of projects in terms of three enablers:

- Clear systemic focus: who, what, when, where, how, why and relevance of plans or responses to events.

- Capability and resources required at any point.

- Will: is intention and resolve to act decisively optimized, stable or declining?

Some questions arise for emergence and other teams such as, 'Will trust in the team disintegrate as complexity rises?' so it can be used to continuously evaluate sustainability in terms of team's Focus, Will and Capability.

Some of the captured data may indicate overlaps with previous team positions or a completed cycle of change following a phase shift, or a lag in a particular dimension such as depth of enactment, for example as the emergence team is still in a 'suck it and see' or 'catch up' mode of operation, or the organization, market or stakeholder community is acting as a constraint in some way such as dithering in decision making or contesting interpretations resulting in stalemate amongst key actors. The broken lines are thus used to indicate some uncertainty, for example, a team in a complex, transitional or morphing mode during a phase

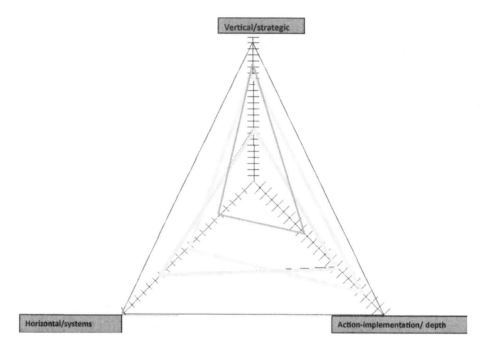

Figure 7.2   Representation of the 3D chart of team development

shift or other dynamics in a VUCA context and 'beg' questions about the next step, 'politics', risk assessment, urgency or timeframes and so on.

Features, advantages and benefits (FAB) of the tool

- it is dynamic, adaptable, integrated, visual and holistic;

- interaction and dynamics across key components is assessed;

- analysis by various methods possible for future action;

- enables analysis of team sustainability, integrity, commitment, gaps in strategy, systems and actions;

- simple and clear – benefits emergence team in terms of avoiding 'mission creep'/value-degeneration/strategic drift;

- gains for tactics and operations too – can be used to address market change (entry/exit) as well as systems and processes.

The team's progress in embodying and embedding intelligence-in-action can be referenced or updated in various timeframes as required and support or other resources supplied as needed or when available.

References

Alutto, J.A., Chan, K.C., Cosier, R.A., Cummings, T.A., Fenoglio, K., Hawawini, G., LeClair, D.R., Milligan, C.H., Roomkin, M., Rucci, A.J., Snyder, E.A., Strawser, J.R., Sullivan, R.S., Williams, J.R. and Zupan, M.A., 2008. Final Report of the AACSB International Impact of Research Task Force. Tampa, FL: AACSB International.

Alvesson, M. and Deetz, S., 2000. *Doing Critical Management Research*. London, UK: Sage.

Argyris, C., 1986. Skilled incompetence, *Harvard Business Review*, September, pp. 74–79.

Argyris, C., 1991. Teaching smart people how to learn, *Harvard Business Review*, May–June, pp. 99–109.

Argyris, C. and Schön, D., 1978. *Organizational Learning: A Theory of Action Perspective*. London, UK: Addison-Wesley.

Argyris, C. and Schön, D., 1996. *Organizational Learning II*. London, UK: Addison-Wesley.

Bean, J.C., 2001. *Engaging Ideas: The Professor's Guide to Integrating Writing, Critical Thinking and Active Learning in the Classroom*. San Francisco, CA: Jossey-Bass.

Blackler, F., Crump, N. and McDonald, S., 1998. Knowledge, organizations and competition. In von Krogh, G., Roos, J. and Kleine, D. eds. *Knowing in Firms*. London, UK: Sage.

Brown, J.S., Collins, A. and Duguid, P., 1995. Situated cognition and the culture of learning, I.L.T.-web, Columbia University. Available at: <http://www.ilt.columbia.edu/ilt/papers/johnBrown.html> [Accessed 10 January 1998].

Cockburn, T.S., 2005. Communities of Commitment: Leadership, Learning Spirals, Teamwork and Emotional Regimes on an MBA, 1997–1999 (available from library of the University of Wales, Cardiff, UK), unpublished thesis.

Cockburn, T. 2006. A Complexity Based Typology of Emotional Regimes in Teams. ITPNZ conference paper, Napier, New Zealand, 28–29 September.

Cockburn, T. and Cockburn-Wootten, C. 2000. Collectivising team Learning. Paper presented at the New Zealand Association for Cooperative Education, Conference, Rotorua, New Zealand, March.

Cockburn, T., Cockburn-Wootten, C, and Simpson, M., 2005. 'That's not fair!' Teaching teamwork relationships and processes, ANZCA conference, Christchurch, New Zealand.

Cockburn, T. and Lewis, T., 1999a. Multi-spiral Learning, 6th Conference of International Centers for Advances in Management, Baton Rouge, USA, July 7–10.

Cockburn, T. and Lewis, T., 1999b. Images of success: Collectivisation of tacit knowledge in work-teams. In Kantarlis, D. ed. Business & Economics for the 21st Century, Vol. III, Worcester, MA: B&ESI, pp. 224–238. Available at: http://www.besiweb.com/OrdCont99.html Last accessed August 10, 2015.

Cockburn, T., Simpson, M. and Cockburn-Wootten, C., 2006. Learning about Teamwork. Available from the Department of Management Communication, Waikato Management School, University of Waikato, New Zealand: Working paper series.

Fineman, S., ed. 1996. *Emotion in Organization*. London, UK: Sage.

Gibbons, M., Limoges, C., Nowotny, H., Schwartzman, S., Scott, P. and Trow, M., 1994. *The New Production of Knowledge: The Dynamics of Science and Research in Contemporary Societies*. London, UK: Sage.

Gill, G. and Bhattacherjee, A., 2009. Whom are we informing? Issues and recommendations for MIS research from an informing sciences perspective. *MIS Quarterly* 33(2), pp. 217–235.

Hessels, L.K. and van Lente, H., 2008. Re-thinking new knowledge production: A literature review and a research agenda. *Research Policy* 37, pp. 740–760.

Hessels, L.K. and van Lente, H., 2010. The mixed blessing of Mode 2 knowledge production. *Science, Technology & Innovation Studies* 6(1), pp. 65–69.

Jung, C.G., 1981. Collected works of C.G. Jung, Volume 9 (Part 1): Archetypes and the collective unconscious. In Adler, G. and Hull, R.F.C. eds. Princeton, NJ: Princeton University Press.

Lewis, T. and Cockburn, T., 2001a. Globalisation and Higher Education: Development of the High Skills Trajectory, European Distance Education Network, 10th Anniversary Conference, Learning Without Limits, 10–13 June, Stockholm, Sweden.

Lewis, T. and Cockburn, T., 2001b. Globalisation and development of the high skills trajectory in higher education. In Kantarlis, D. ed. *Global Business and Economics Anthology*. Worcester, MA: B&ESI.

Martin, C., 1999. *Net Future: 7 Cybertrends That Will Drive Your Business, Create New Wealth, and Define Your Future*. New York, NY: McGraw-Hill.

Meyer, J.H.F. and Land, R., 2003. Threshold concepts and troublesome knowledge (1): linkages to ways of thinking and practicing. In Rust, C. ed. *Improving Student Learning – Ten Years On*. Oxford, UK: OCSLD.

Meyer, J.H.F., Land, R. and Davies, P., 2006. Implications of threshold concepts for course design and evaluation. In Meyer, J.H.F. and Land, R. eds. *Overcoming*

Barriers to Student Understanding: Threshold Concepts and Troublesome Knowledge. London, UK and New York, NY: Routledge.

Nonaka, I., 1991. The knowledge creating company. *Harvard Business Review*, November–December, pp. 96–104.

Nonaka I., 1994. A dynamic theory of organizational knowledge creation. *Organization Science* 5(1), pp. 14–37.

Nonaka, I., ed. 2005. *Knowledge Management: Critical Perspectives on Business and Management, Volume 2*. New York, NY: Routledge.

Nonaka, I. and Takeuchi, H., 1995. *The Knowledge-Creating Company, How Japanese Companies Create the Dynamics of Innovation*. Oxford, UK: Oxford University Press.

Nonaka, I. and Teece, D., eds. 2001. *Managing Industrial Knowledge*. London, UK: Sage.

Nonaka, I., Toyama, R. and Nagata, A., 2000. A firm as a knowledge-creating entity: A new perspective on the theory of the firm. *Industrial and Corporate Change* 9(1), pp. 1–20.

Pfeffer, J. and Fong, C.T., 2002. The end of business schools? Less success than meets the eye. *Academy of Management Learning & Education* 1(1), pp. 78–95.

Revans, R., 1996. *The ABC of Action Learning*. London: Lemos & Crane.

Schön, D., 1994. Teaching artistry through reflection-in-action. In Tsoukas, H. ed. *New Thinking In Organizational Behaviour*. Oxford, UK: Butterworth-Heinemann.

Schön, D., 1995. The new scholarship requires a new epistemology. *Change*, November/December, 27, 6.

Schön, D., 1996. Organisational learning: The core issues. Conference paper 10: Organisational Learning. London, UK: London Office of Public Management.

Senge, P.M., 1990. *The Fifth Discipline: The Art and Practice of the Learning Organization*. New York, NY: Doubleday.

Senge, P.M. et al., eds. 1994. *The Fifth Discipline Fieldbook. Strategies and Tools for Building a Learning Organization*. New York, NY: Doubleday.

Simpson, M., Cockburn-Wootten, C. and Cockburn, T., 2005. Resistance; the unexpected consequences of implementing change, International Conference on Case Study teaching and learning, University of Auckland, pp. 1–14, New Zealand.

Smith, P.A.C. and Cockburn, T., 2013. *Dynamic Leadership Models for Global Business: Enhancing Digitally Connected Environments*. Hershey, PA: IGI Global.

Smith, P.A.C., and Cockburn, T., eds. 2014. *Impact of Emerging Digital Technologies on Leadership in Global Business*. Hershey, PA: IGI Global.

Sparrow, J., 1998. *Knowledge in Organizations*. London, UK: Sage.

Tuckman B., 1965. Developmental sequence in small groups. *Psychological Bulletin* 63, pp. 384–399.

von Krogh, G., Roos, J. and Kleine, D., 1998. *Knowing in Firms*. London, UK: Sage.

Wenger, E., 1998. *Communities of Practice*. New York, NY: Cambridge University Press.

Chapter 8
Digital technology and emerging teams

Introduction

Readers should note that this chapter is not intended to be prescriptive, but rather is intended to provide familiarization with relevant digital technology. Digital technology is evolving at a frantic pace; by the time this chapter goes to press, some of its recommendations may be out of date, and readers are cautioned to re-establish the veracity of statements concerning particular digital devices or software. Each subsection in this chapter addresses digital technology relevant to some form of emergence team activity; some activities are sufficiently broad that the technology described in more than one subsection may be relevant. Note that no particular subsection is devoted to the application of mobile technology since, given the widespread acceptance of social media, team members will be very familiar with both the technology and its potential to facilitate any of their activities. The Internet provides a rich and up-to-date source for digital information and technical reviews; readers are recommended to search there for current information prior to making important decisions.

At an early team meeting, team members and the team leader might hold a dialogue concerning the merits of having the team leader assume the role of digital technology 'watchdog'. The team leader would then assume day-to-day responsibility for ensuring that such digital technology as the team is using, or plans to use, is appropriate.

Digital security must also be a high concern for the team leader and team members when such technology will be used. Smith and Cockburn (2014, p. 215–254) provide details of a variety of digital security concerns; familiarity with these chapters will be very helpful to the team in further discussions with the organization's IT department. Such discussions are high priority when digital technology of any kind will be used by the team, and must focus on the security ground rules that the organization already has in place or needs to implement, given the technology that the team plans to utilize.

Although aspects of digital technologies may be treated independently in this section, the reader is cautioned that as noted by Smith and Cockburn (2013, p. 31) 'digital technologies often display the greatest synergy when used in combination in holistic fashion, and digital technologies should not be segmented without situational consideration'. Digital technologies will have the greatest impact when organizational leaders, prior to the introduction of emergence teams, encourage a digitally aware environment by, as described by Smith and Cockburn (2013, p. 32):

- cultivating an organizational culture where digital experimentation is encouraged;

- encouraging and applying digital leadership throughout the organization (Smith and Cockburn, 2013);

- introducing technology across the organization for improved communication, sharing and interaction;

- recommending practitioners limit or 'power down' their digital involvement to avoid 'digital fatigue and burn-out';

- utilizing automation technology to improve efficiency;

- encouraging learning communities, Communities of Practice (COP) (Wenger, 2000; Wenger, 2001; Wenger et al., 2002), and Communities of Innovation (CoInv) (Smith and Coakes, 2007).

Process models and digital technology

In Chapter 4, four step-wise process models are described to address a team leader's role; however the models are generic and in Chapter 6 we strongly recommend adopting them to address the problem with which the team has been tasked. Smith and Cockburn (2014) show how the four step-wise process models presented in Chapter 4 may be augmented to include the impact of the various new and emerging digital technologies, and a part of this chapter (Chapter 8) is devoted to discussing how these emerging digital technologies may be integrated into these models, and the resulting potential impact from the team members' point of view. According to Smith and Cockburn (2014) these include a very broad range of digital technologies.

As emphasized in Chapter 4, the first process step demands that emergence team members and the team leader possess excellent clarity and understanding of their team and leadership role – what the leader and the team is expected to achieve. This target expectation forms the team's scoreboard and the leader's and team members' success will be judged on results versus this scoreboard. This holds true as the leader or team members attempt to introduce emerging digital technologies into their team leadership and teamwork practices. If the role does not specifically include the potential introduction of emerging digital technologies into the team's project environment, great care must be exercised to demonstrate that such digital technology as is introduced can be seen to be directly linked to achieving the essential elements of the team leader's and the team's role.

As noted above, we recommend adopting the team leader's four-step process models to address the problem with which the team has been tasked. When this substitution has been accepted, Figure 4.1 in Chapter 4 (Process Step 2) helps identify the Cynefin environment, and Figure 4.2 in Chapter 4 (Process Step 3) relates to the 'probe, sense and respond' steps in the Cynefin framework. In this case an enabler would be the response that the team (and the team leader) believes might help mitigate the problem.

Smith and Cockburn (2013) strongly emphasize the importance of Process Step 4 where, based on their experience in Process Steps 1 through 3, the team leader and the team members evaluate their actual roles for relevance given the goal structures and rules underlying their specified target role. Should they discover a possible mismatch, they must seek to have their target role reviewed and revised as appropriate; this holds true particularly when the introduction of emerging digital technologies seems appropriate.

Social media based on mobile technology has had a very broad impact and it is highly likely that all the emergence team members have been exposed to it prior to joining the team. Assuming that their experience has been positive, team members will agree with Smith and Cockburn (2014) who claim that mobile phones and tablets have significant potential for enhancing team learning and reflection, especially in Process Steps 2 and 3. Maglajlic and Helic (2012) identify a high correlation between the intensity of communication and the learning outcomes. Research by Aberdeen Group (2012) indicates that there is widespread use of mobile phones and tablets for knowledge sharing and learning. According to these authors, major drivers for using mobile technology are an enhanced learning experience plus improved learning administration. As is typical of complexity, mobile technology is co-evolving with learners and their needs, and this will be true for emergence team activities.

Analytics is another emerging digital technology that may have relevance in Process Step 2 activities, although emergence team members may not be familiar with it. Bersin (2013) defines the word 'Analytics' as the systematic discovery of meaningful patterns in data to support decision making. Analytics is typically the process of turning *large quantities* of data into information that is digestible and actionable. Analytics includes reporting and Dashboarding (Levy, 2011; IBM, 2013; Dashboards, 2013); predictive analyses; and scenario-modelling.

Dashboards (2013) are becoming increasingly highly prized for Business Intelligence (BI) and they have potential to assist team members in Process Steps 2 and 3; however high development cost may be a deterrent. In the 1980s, Executive Information Systems (EIS) performed a similar service but today's Dashboards are far more interactive and usable for the current dynamic business requirements. Modern Dashboards have the capability to present data and information in summary which makes them very powerful tools for BI, although the question of how to calculate the return on a Dashboard investment can be difficult. Many of the charts used in older EIS were similar to those in use in today's Dashboards. This is because user needs have not changed much over time. However, what has changed is the availability of more sophisticated technology and potentially more sophisticated users (team members). Modern Dashboards meet business needs in a practical and actionable way, whereby quick snapshots of the big picture are made available whilst detail is also available. Dashboards would provide 'at-a-glance' views of key performance indicators (F, W, C) relevant to the problem that the emergence team is addressing. The most useful Dashboards for Process Steps 2 and 3 would be designed to highlight for team members the problem timelines, historical narratives and values for performance evaluators (F, W, C).

Spreadsheets might also be used as an alternative to the dashboard. Spreadsheets are typically Microsoft Excel documents. Their advantage is that they are easier to use, and they make available detailed numbers, which team members can then analyse using their own calculations. Unfortunately, the spreadsheet is often too detailed to give a fast comprehensive overview of Process Step 2 data; however, given their ease of development, spreadsheets could provide an attractive tool in Process Step 2 activity.

Scorecards to provide 'at-a-glance' visualization of the status of Focus, Will and Capability in Process Step 2 have been used in many practical situations (Tosey and Smith, 1999) and could be developed for use by emergence team members based on the kind of appraisal set out in Smith and Cockburn (2013, p. 49 and p. 265). Such scorecards, for rough visualization of the status of Focus, Will and Capability are based on transferring the numerical outcomes from an appraisal on to three vectors each scaled from 0 to 10 (Tosey and Smith, 1999). The use of scorecards implies the use of surveys for the appraisal. Also, surveys in their own right may be used very profitably in Process Step 2 to help ascertain how others view the manner in which the team's role is being discharged, and to gauge the effect of enablers. Online surveys are easy to assemble and may be readily distributed, collected and analysed. A primer on survey design for the Internet is provided at Survey (2014), and many commercial software 'do it yourself' systems are available.

Given that emergence team members have been nominated by individuals across the organization, it is highly likely that the team members belong to one or more social networks. These networks offer team members access to potentially useful information in Process Step 2, for example in regard to enablers that others have found useful, or the availability of Focus and Capability enhancement opportunities, or simply to gain organizational 'savvy' in all areas of practice. In assessing organizational Capability, it is noteworthy, that Arinze (2012) has asserted that E-Collaboration has come of age in the last decade and the presence of such software in an organization to bring together groups of interested practitioners would indicate heightened Capability.

The third process step, as explained earlier, involves the team leader and team members very frequently cycling through a succession of activities in an experiential learning cycle. The emphasis in this case is on personal learning and reflection; comments regarding emerging digital technologies recommended in regard to Process Steps 1 and 2 above are appropriate in this step. This learning and reflection will typically be a team activity; that is, it will be carried out in the company of learning partners. As Smith and Cockburn (2013, p. 35 and pp. 46–47) explain at length, action learning is very well suited to the type of learning and reflection that is fundamental to this step. The extent to which team members wish to apply digital technology to broaden the circle of their learning partners, or facilitate dialogue where these partners are situated at a distance, is a matter that the team members must decide. The emergence of ubiquitous digital interconnectivity for social networks has provided a ready means by which public and private conversations may take place across an organization. This is critical to the widespread sharing and generation of knowledge, and to learning and reflection in general. This widespread digital interconnectivity for social networks has already provided a means for online action learning (VAL) to be carried out at arm's length between an action learning group's participants. Dickenson et al. (2010) report findings from their research exploring online action learning

(VAL) as an emerging variety of action learning. These authors note that VAL provides value by bringing together geographically dispersed individuals within and across organizations, and possibly across time. At the beginning of this research there appeared to be little evidence of VAL being widely used, although face-to-face action learning was well known and practised. Although there was considerable interest expressed by educationalists and practitioners in VAL, there was a lack of understanding regarding how to go about it. However, the research findings revealed more practice than was anticipated and demonstrated that VAL is a distinct variety of action learning, characterized by its virtual, non-f2f nature, and that it has its own strengths and weaknesses. Dickinson et al. (2010) provide a classification of VAL, plus consideration of the theoretical questions associated with its practice, and they explore its potential in the light of emerging technologies. These authors conclude that, like action learning, VAL is not singular, but takes a variety of forms, each with distinct characteristics, advantages and shortcomings. It is further reported in a study by Plack et al. (2010) that most of the students engaged in VAL were able to demonstrate reflection on complex clinical issues. A later subsection in this chapter provides further details regarding VAL design and implementation. Some further practical pointers may be gleaned from work addressing leadership in virtual team environments by Pauleen (2003).

Smith and Cockburn (2013) recommend that each team member keep a personal reflective journal that may be used at a later date to help in selecting enablers or for resolving other performance issues. In the past, such a journal was laborious to compile by long-hand, and very difficult to search when one wished to locate a particular incident; digitization has revolutionized the keeping of such a journal and also the capability to search it using keywords (tags). There are many commercial digitized 'diary' products on the market; such a well-known app is Day One (2013) which is usable via mobile devices, and which has key word searchability. Such a digital journal may also be readily backed-up for security purposes by, for example, using Dropbox (2013). Dropbox also facilitates sharing the journal and ensures that the journal is available on all a user's digital devices.

The question of whether team members could adopt cloud computing in relation to any of the dynamic leadership models described in this chapter to a large extent depends on: (a) the ready availability of cloud computing to realize the capabilities of the emerging technology being applied to the model; or (b) the policies and capabilities of the IT department of the team's organization, or both (a) and (b). There is no shortage of hype regarding cloud computing, but CNBC

(2011) provides clarification that cuts through the rhetoric. For example this source claims that 'cloud computing can be grasped on its basic level – anytime, anywhere computing – without the user ever having to know much about the technology' and, 'In simplest terms, cloud computing involves delivering hosted services over the Internet. The *service end* is where the data or software is stored and the *user end* is a single person or company network.' Cloud computing offers cost savings and enhanced ease of use, but as CNBC (2011) cautions, 'By using cloud computing, a company opens a door into its data and that door is an attractive target for attacks.'

Teamwork and digital technology

Immediate relevant feedback on team performance is critical, and if Dashboards (2013) are considered too ambitious for this purpose, surveys may be developed that will provide simplified visualization of the team's work status founded on 'how others view the manner in which the team or a team member has carried out the work'. Online surveys may be easily assembled, distributed, collected and analysed in timely fashion. A primer on Internet survey design is provided at Survey (2013) and various commercial 'Do it yourself' software systems are available.

The benefit of using action learning to facilitate the emergence team's problem exploration has been explained in previously. We emphasize that, when necessary, online action learning may be carried out at arm's length (VAL) between team members (IFAL, 2013). However, if it is feasible and more straightforward for the emergence team to carry out the action learning process face-to-face, rather than online, then we would recommend the face-to-face approach.

Virtual action leaning (VAL)

As noted above and in Chapter 1, action learning may be carried out successfully in a virtual environment (DeWolfe Waddill et al., 2006; Waddill, 2006). This e-learning approach to action learning is typically termed VAL. The article by DeWolfe Waddill et al. (2006) describes three action-based, constructivist e-learning strategies. These leading-edge, proven, innovative delivery methods are claimed to be appropriate for both educational institutions and business organizations. The most appropriate of these strategies for application by an emergence team is the Managerial Learning Model based on research by Rungtusanatham et al.

(2004) that provides an appropriate e-learning environment for the promotion of higher-order thinking/learning.

Based on the research of DeWolfe Waddill et al. (2006) the face-to-face action learning approach described previously may be successfully ported into an online structure with a few provisos identified by these authors. For example, it is prudent at an initial stage of e-learning design, for emergence team members to collaborate with the team leader (acting as an action e-learning adviser) to develop online behavioural norms. These norms should be very specific (Brindle and Levesque, 2000) and should include rules of online etiquette intended to sustain respectful online interaction. These rules of interaction must be maintained to ensure a healthy context for learning. The team members also need familiarization with the formal process of action learning; this familiarization would be necessary whether the team was undertaking face-to-face action learning or an e-learning variant. If it is feasible and more straightforward for the emergence team to carry out the action learning process face-to-face, rather than online, then we would recommend the face-to-face approach.

Interviewing and digital technology

Team members will certainly be meeting across the organization with individuals who have been nominated to provide first-hand source material with regard to the problem with which the team has been tasked. Interviewing prospective business employees using digital technology is now widespread although training of the operators is required. This technology provides consistency in interviews and also provides the opportunity to record the interview. This makes available encrypted digital recording, and simplified storage and playback to all team members (Shratz, 2014; AirForce News, 2014; Dictate, 2014).

AirForceNews (2014) highlights insights that legitimize the technology for formal interviewing; both UK civil and Air Force police, according to this article, are now embracing Digital Audio Visual Interview Equipment commonly referred to as 'Digital AV' to tape record interviews with crime suspects and other persons of interest. These interviews are carried out using touch screen technology and instant, encrypted digital recording with DVD playback. Computing (2014) explains how the police utilize digital recording and playback to speed up their interview processes, because digital recording enables interviews to be recorded straight on to a secure digital network; this also improves its accessibility for other police departments.

Dictate (2014) claims that the digital voice recorder has become an essential tool of the journalist; further general information is provided by Impact (2014) and Wave (2014). Dictate (2014) also claims that 'a digital voice recorder is essential for recording sound bites for either later playback on a website, or to be used in a radio/online report, or for reference when transcribing research into the final piece'.

Technology points to watch for, according to Dictate (2014):

- must have compatibility with both Mac and Windows systems;

- must ensure there are no proprietary software requirements for retrieving the audio from the digital voice recorder (that is, plug and play);

- mandatory recording in MP3 at the highest possible bit rate, for example minimum 320kbps or 256 kbps;

- since most recorders now have gigabytes of storage memory, storage should not be a concern on modern machines;

- rechargeable batteries are nice to have but are not a necessity.

Dictate (2014) highly recommends the Olympus range of digital voice recorders. According to this source The WS series recorders are superb, and their audio pickup is phenomenal, as are all the mid- to high-end Olympus recorders (see some details below).

Olympus WS-812

- small, lightweight digital voice recorder with excellent audio pickup;

- runs off one x rechargeable AAA or 1x alkaline AAA;

- records in PCM (uncompressed WAV [higher than CD quality], MP3 and WMA audio formats);

- Mac and Windows compatible – plug and play – no software required;

- power-up is instant;

- has 4Gb of built-in storage that is expandable via a microSD/microSDHC card;

- internal storage records for a maximum 33 hours in MP3 256kbps mode; six hours in PCM WAV mode; 65 hours in STXQ (high-quality WMA mode).

According to Dictate (2014), an excellent alternative is the Olympus LM-3.

Olympus LM-3

- slightly larger than the WS;

- both WS-812 and LM-3 have 4Gb of built-in memory, expandable via a microSH/microSDHC card;

- both WS-812 and LM-3 record in PCM WAV, MP3 and WAV audio formats;

- both have a zoom mic with outstanding audio pickup for any situation;

- Mac and Windows compatible – plug and play – no software required;

- upgradeable via Olympus firmware updates, slightly slower power-up than WS series.

The most significant advantage is the availability of excellent zoom mics.

Digital interviewing, where a potential candidate is screened for an organizational position, is now widespread (Schratz, 2014), and if the HR department for the organization associated with the emergence team utilizes digital interviewing, this department would be an excellent source of information regarding recorders and recording technique and so on.

Malamed (2015) details some very useful common-sense digital options to facilitate interviewing, and other emergence team activities. On the basis of this author's recommendations, team members are strongly advised to record their interviews with employees who are nominated to recount their stories, since this will provide improved accuracy and will enable the interviewer to better concentrate on what the interviewee is saying.

Interviewing/team activity and digital technology

Malamed (2015) claims that a variety of tools are available to facilitate interviewing, but cautions that an interviewer must always make sure that the interviewee has given written permission for the interview to be recorded. Malamed (2015) recommends the following:

- When mounted on a tripod, a small pocket camera, video recorder, or high-quality camera, for example the ZoomQ2HD, will suffice.

- A good quality external microphone is necessary to provide clarity if the interview is to be transcribed – an omnidirectional mic should be used if the interviewer and the interviewee are sharing the same mic, and unidirectional mics if each has their own.

- Audio may be directly recorded into a laptop computer; Audacity (2015) is a popular recording and editing process.

- Skype may be used for remote interviewing; but Skype does not provide recording options; however Pamela records Skype video and audio on a PC, and Total Recorder (2015) records audio from any source on a PC.

- Webconfrev (2015) lists numerous meeting room, conference call and webinar online sites that are available where video and sound recordings may be made for downloading to local devices or for distribution, or to facilitate team meetings and online action learning (VAL).

- Interviews may also be captured using Screen Recordings:
    - ScreenCastle (2015);
    - ScreenFlow (2015) for Mac-based usage.

Malamed (2015) points out that if the interviewer wants to share media files with other team members, he or she will need somewhere to store them, and suggests that cloud storage services are a good option. Another convenient option is Dropbox.

'Oral history' and digital technology

The oral history movement – capturing family stories from older family members – is now growing rapidly thanks partly to the arrival of cheap, easy-to-use digital recorders, and AskJack (2015) in relation to capturing oral histories claims that the voice recorder market is under pressure from mobile phones, which do a reasonable job without the recording person having to carry an extra device around.

Dictation products are intended to record voices either for memo-taking or later transcription. The main benefits of voice recorders are their long recording times and long battery life. The principle audio requirement is for clarity rather than fidelity, and therefore mono sound is acceptable; a bit rate of 192 kbps in Microsoft's WMA (WMedia Audio) format counts as superb high quality. To reduce background noise, cut-off filters may be utilized. For interviews, voice recorders work best when they are operated fairly close to the interviewee's mouth. Dictation machines may also include small loudspeakers so that the interviewer can listen to the recording. These machines record MP3 files, which can produce excellent sound quality at high bit-rates (up to 320 kbps) and the files will play back on virtually every device. The main suppliers in this market are Olympus and Sony.

AskJack (2015) advises that a good quality dictation machine is the Sony ICD-PX312, which has 2Gb of built-in storage and can record to MP3 files. This machine also takes SD memory cards (not supplied), and can be connected to a PC's USB port. According to AskJack (2015) the Olympus VN-713PC is also worth considering. This is another WMA/MP3 mono voice recorder with USB connectivity, but it has 4Gb of built-in storage plus a kick-stand and a microSD card slot instead of an SD slot. It also has noise cancellation to reduce the effect of background noises such as air conditioning. Both of these recorders will capture clear voices and have 'scene' commands in order to handle different recording situations,

Sophisticated story capture and digital technology

Gordon and Ganesan (2015) assert that while storytelling has long been recognized as an important part of effective knowledge management in organizations (Boyce, 1996; Snowden, 1999), knowledge management technologies have generally not distinguished between stories and other types of discourse. They go on to describe a new type of technological support for storytelling that involves automatically capturing the stories that people tell to each other in conversations. In their paper, Gordon and Ganesen (2015) focus on a key enabling technology to support their vision of story-based knowledge management via the automated identification and extraction of stories in conversational speech. These authors describe two types of story capture systems:

1. *Passive story extraction systems*: where the conversations that people have among themselves are monitored for the presence of stories that are then automatically extracted. For example, a Personal Story Monitor would simply listen to the words that employees speak in the course of their normal telephone conversations with other people, and extract and archive the audio segments of those conversations that were automatically judged to be stories. The passive story extraction process results in significant privacy concerns; one solution is to ask users to review and approve the audio clips associated with extracted stories before they are archived. Gordon and Ganesen (2015) describe, as an example of a passive story extraction system, their own attempt to create a story recognition process using statistical text-classification techniques.

2. *Active story extraction systems*: where employees would call a specific Telephone Exchange Server and would be prompted to tell their story. At the completion of a user's story, the audio recording of the story would be automatically archived along with the set of file identification words that could automatically be recognized from the users' story.

Speech tecognition digital technology

The overall principle of voice recognition software is to allow the user to dictate words into a microphone that are then transformed into text in a word processor or into commands for an app without having to key them in from a computer keyboard. The capability to automatically translate a verbal story into text has obvious major benefits to emergence team members when they are conducting interviews. List (2015) and Snow (2015) provide comparative reviews of speech recognition systems.

Speech recognition tools are available in Microsoft Office and Windows; however, for serious usage a more powerful software system will be required. Noffsinger (2015) explains that voice recognition computer software has been in development since the 1950s, but only in the past three or four years has it become available and affordable for use by the general public. Unfortunately there is a major technical shortcoming in that most speech recognition systems must be trained to recognize the speech idiosyncrasies of a particular individual before the system will produce an accurate transcription of that individual's dictation. Since an emergence team will interview a wide variety of storytellers this obstruction presents an insurmountable hurdle at this time; however, the capability to accurately recognize the speech patterns of many different individuals is planned for most systems at some later date according to Noffsinger (2015). Voice recognition software typically allows the user to dictate using a normal speaking pattern; however as noted above, voice recognition software requires the user to invest some time adapting (training) the programme to recognize his or her individual voice and speaking idiosyncrasies. The system usually then requires the user to correct recognition errors made by the system. This continued cycle of correction and learning for the system results in improved word-recognition accuracy rates. Noffsinger (2015) claims that newer voice recognition software allows for multiple users, although each user must train the computer to recognize his or her individual speech patterns.

According to Noffsinger (2015) and Dragon (2015), NaturallySpeaking, developed by Nuance and produced by Dragon Systems, Inc. is the best-known speech recognition system available. NuanceDragon Systems Inc. has been developing voice recognition software since 1982 and Noffsinger (2015) quotes *PC World* that NaturallySpeaking's word-recognition accuracy rate is 98 per cent and it is able to recognize speech at up to 160 words per minute. It has a built-in vocabulary of 230,000 words, with space for the user to add another 25,000 of their own words. NaturallySpeaking also allows the computer to read the dictation out loud for proofreading.

Cohen (2015) provides a very helpful review of speech recognition technology but essentially limits the review to Mac-based products. This commentator asserts that speech recognition is a technology that took a long time to become popular, but 'in today's world of smartphones, wearables, and smart home devices, it's suddenly everywhere' and 'we are surrounded by gadgets capable of understanding the spoken word like never before'. This commentator goes on to remind us that Dragon NaturallySpeaking software, developed by Nuance, is in Version 13 for Windows and Version 4 for Mac (renamed Dragon Dictate), so it has been popular for a considerable period. Nuance is the dominant player in the speech recognition field, and its technology is a fundamental part of Apple's Siri and similar products from other companies. Cohen (2015) claims that there are plenty of reasons to consider a full-blown version of this software for your computer; however, although Dragon is very impressive (Mac-based Dragon Dictate 4 is nearly word perfect with an accuracy of 99 per cent), Cohen cautions that 'frankly, if the only reason you're looking at speech recognition software is the ability to do some basic dictation, you're probably better off with your system's built-in software'.

Digital technology: Conclusions and future trends

Throughout this chapter, the authors have been discussing how emergence team members may learn to figure out and better achieve their role by utilizing emerging digital technologies as appropriate. Social media was once the exclusive domain of digital gurus; however, Twitter, Facebook and other tools are present in everyone's kit bag and 'We are seeing an increased demand for social savvy candidates across the business – from human resources to product to customer service' (Holmes, 2013). It must be noted though that digital technologies provide both credits and debits. The biggest debit associated with these technologies is digital fatigue (Kenyon, 2013). As Deiser and Newton (2013) point out, 'The Social media has created an ocean of information. We are drowning in a never-ending flood of e-mails, tweets, Facebook updates, RSS feeds, and more that's often hard to navigate.' These authors propose that individuals must become proficient not only in the software itself, but also in using the settings that filter important from unimportant information. Unfortunately, this is only a partial solution, since fundamental to social media is social interaction, and a team member must decide on whether and when to comment and/or reply, and in what fashion to apply the information. This is more time consuming than it might appear, since most of such information requires assessment of its source, authenticity and credibility. In addition, to remain a legitimate team player in this social dialogue, there is considerable pressure to respond immediately in this social process of creating meaning. Although individuals from the millennial generation are more adept at handling such rapid digital dialogue, there remain questions regarding their ability to reflect and make meaning from such exchanges (Barry, 2013), and indeed their growing antagonism to digital media (Grensing-Pophal, 2013). This digital fatigue problem is likely only to grow worse in the future, and ultimately the answer lies with the emergence team leader and the team members developing appropriate discipline and working guidelines.

Developing an appropriate global business perspective among emergence team members implies that 'one needs to enhance one's understanding of the social, political, technological and environmental forces that are shaping our existence and our children's future, including an understanding of the links between us and others throughout the world' (Smith and Cockburn, 2013, pp. 258–259). There was a time when this involved onerous undertakings to search for relevant information in books, journals, magazines and newspapers through an organization's library or information service. Progress on the Internet has meant that much of the searching and indexing on given topics are now done for team members by commercial organizations to which they can subscribe. In addition, search engine capability provides them with quick and easy access to ad hoc information searches as required, and 'clipping' software such as Evernote (2013) and 'sharing' software such as Dropbox (2013) facilitate their personalizing retention and sharing of information. Linkedin (2013) through its general postings, networks and discussion groups also provides an excellent means for team members to stay up to date on global topics and to pose questions as appropriate. It is reasonable to suppose that such services will become even more user friendly and search question-focused in the future. The increasing use of mobile devices will certainly encourage this trend.

The relevance of a number of digital technologies to the dynamic leadership models proposed by Smith and Cockburn (2013) were treated in the first subsections. Three topics that were unexplored hold much promise for facilitating the development of agile leaders capable of functioning in VUCA environments and emergence teams. These are Games, Simulations and Elearning. The successful application of Game and Simulations technologies to leadership development is not new (Smith and Levinson, 1996), but their growing sophistication promises much for the future, and emergence teams are urged to follow emerging trends and products. Ballance (2013) supports this recommendation, noting that corporations and other organizations around the world are recognizing that games promote cognitive reasoning and information retention, and that modern games are advanced, immersive and engaging. Another topic that has particular relevance to the broader topics of organizational learning and emergence team development is e-learning, both in its synchronous and asynchronous forms. E-learning is a broadly inclusive term that describes educational technology that electronically or technologically supports learning and/or teaching. This again is a topic that has a long history, but it is one where enhancements continue to be made, particularly in regard to mobile delivery. Zhang (2003) provides a broad and detailed, if somewhat dated, overview of the subject, and Wikipedia (Elearning, 2013) and Venkatesh (2015) provide comprehensive current accounts.

Effective and efficient networking and collaboration within organizations and between individuals are critical success factors for achieving global competitive business advantage, and today's business environments demand updated tools and practices reflecting these factors, particularly in globalized environments (Hypia and Pekkola, 2011). It is concluded that an understanding and adoption of the dynamic models detailed in this book together with a broad familiarity with application of the emerging digital technologies highlighted in this chapter will satisfy the critical success factors criteria, and will be highly beneficial not only for emergence teams but also for the organization in general.

References

Aberdeen Group 2012. Analyst insight: Learning on the move by the Aberdeen Group. Available at: <http://www.netdimensions.com/downloads/analyst-reports/rp-aberdeen.pdf> [Retrieved 9 October 2013].

AirForceNews 2014. Available at: <http://www.businesssystemsuk.co.uk/a-recording-revolution-digital-interviewing-technology> [Retrieved 10 December 2014].

Arinze, B., 2012. E-Research collaboration in Academia and Industry. *International Journal of e-Collaboration* 8(2), pp. 1–13.

Askjack 2015. Available at: <http://www.theguardian.com/technology/askjack/2013/mar/21/which-voice-recorder-capture-parents-history> [Retrieved 27 April 2015].

Audacity 2015. Available at: <http://podcast-software-review.toptenreviews.com/audacity-review.html> [Retrieved 24 April 2015].

Ballance, C., 2013. Use of games in training: Interactive experiences that engage us to learn. *Industrial and Commercial Training* 45(4), pp. 218–221.

Barry, E., 2013. Generation distracted by multiple digital devices. Available at: <http://www.news.com.au/technology/generation-distracted-by-multiple-digital-devices/story-e6frfrnr-1226732537892#!> [Retrieved 15 October 2013].

Bersin, J., 2013. Deloitte Research Bulletin. Talent analytics – from small data to big data. Available at: <http://marketing.bersin.com/talent-analytics-small-data-to-big-data.html> [Retrieved 9 October 2013].

Brindle, J. and Levesque, L., 2000. Bridging the gap: Challenges and prescriptions for interactive distance education. *Journal of Management Education* 24(4), pp. 445–457.

Boyce, M.E., 1996. Organizational story and storytelling: A critical review. *Journal of Organizational Change Management* 9(5), pp. 5–26.

Cavaleri S. and Seivert S., 2005. *Knowledge Leadership*. Burlington, MA: Elsevier.

CNBC 2011. Cloud computing 101: Learning the basics. Available at: <http://www.cnbc.com/id/43077233> [Retrieved 12 October 2013].

Cohen, S., 2015. Nuance Dragon Dictate 4 is nearly word perfect (review). Available at: <http://venturebeat.com/2014/08/22/nuance-dragon-dictate-4-is-nearly-word-perfect-review/> [Retrieved 28 April 2015].

Computing 2014. Available at: <http://www.computing.co.uk/ctg/news/2023897/digital-recording-technology-assist-police-inquiries> [Retrieved 10 December 2014].

Dashboards 2013. Available at: <http://en.wikipedia.org/wiki/Dashboard_%28business%29> [Retrieved 9 October 2013].

Day One 2013. Journal/Diary. Available at: <https://itunes.apple.com/ca/app/day-one-journal-diary/id421706526?mt=8> [Retrieved 10 October 2013].

Deiser, R. and Newton, S., 2013. Six social-media skills every leader needs. Available at: <https://www.mckinseyquarterly.com/Strategy/Innovation/Six_social-media_skills_every_leader_needs_3056> [Retrieved 15 October 2013].

De Wolfe Waddill, D., Milter, R. and Defillippi, R., 2006. Strategies for an action-based e-learning experience. Available at: <http://files.eric.ed.gov/fulltext/ED492728.pdf? [Retrieved 8 May 2015].

Dickenson, M., Burgoyne J. and Pedler, M., 2010. Virtual action learning: Practices and challenges. *Action Learning: Research and Practice* 7(1), pp. 59–72.

Dictate 2014. Available at: <http://dictate.uk.com/2012/09/journalist-essential-tool-journalism-voice-recorder-digital/> [Retrieved 10 December 2014].

Dragon 2015. Available at: http://wordprocessing.about.com/od/choosingsoftware/fr/DragonNaturallySpeaking10.htm [Retrieved 29 April 2015].

Dropbox 2013. Dropbox for business. Available at: <https://www.dropbox.com/business?_tk=adwords&_kw=dropboxle&_net=g&_ad=33733502862l1t1&_camp=Search%3A%20Brand%20%22Dropbox%22%20-%20CA&gclid=CI-iyoq9j7oCFfBaMgodzEUAYQ> [Retrieved 10 October 2013].

Elearning 2013. Available at: <http://en.wikipedia.org/wiki/E-learning> [Retrieved 14 October 2013].

Evernote 2013. Available at: <evernote.com> [Retrieved 13 October 2013].

Gordon, A.S. and Ganesan, K., 2015. Automated story capture from conversational speech. Available at: <http://people.ict.usc.edu/~gordon/publications/KCAP05.PDF> [Retrieved 12 April 2015].

Grensing-Pophal, L. 2013. What does the digital generation's tech fatigue mean for content providers? Available at: <http://www.econtentmag.com/Articles/News/News-Feature/What-Does-the-Digital-Generations-Tech-Fatigue-Mean-for-Content-Providers-91694.htm#!> [Retrieved 14 October 2013].

Holmes, R., 2013. The social media manager is dead. Long live social media. Available at: <http://management.fortune.cnn.com/2013/10/01/social-media-manager/#!> [Retrieved 15 October 2013].

Hyypia, M. and Pekkola, S., 2011. Interaction challenges in leadership and performance management in developing a network environment. *Journal of Advances in Management Research* 8(1), pp. 85–98.

IBM 2013. Extending business intelligence with dashboards. Available at: <https://www14.software.ibm.com/webapp/iwm/web/signup.do?source=swg-BA_WebOrganic&S_PKG=ov4005&form=170&S_CMP=Google-Display-SWG-Cognos-WP-3099&csr=wwus_cognosdashboard-20130716&cm=k&cr=google&ct=101KR81W&S_TACT=101KR81W&ck=dashboard_best_practices&cmp=101KR&mkwid=sZ8lBwI56_32246842748_43246d30503&gclid=COj34vSOj7oCFYZaMgodVk0AeA> [Retrieved 10 October 2013].

IFAL 2013. Where action-learning comes from and where it's going. Available at <http://ifal.org.uk/ action-learning/ origins-of-action-learning/> [Retrieved 10 October 2013].

Impact 2014. Available at: <https://answers.yahoo.com/question/index?qid=20101025134056AA16T5z> [Retrieved 10 December 2014].

Kenyon, K. 2013. Fighting digital fatigue. Available at: <http://www.whipsmartcontent.com/2013/09/06/fighting-digital-fatigue/> [Retrieved 15 October 2013].

Levy, D., 2011. Dashboards best practices. Available at: <http://issuu.com/gmerp/docs/dashboards-best-practices> [Retrieved 10 October 2013].

LinkedIn 2013. Available at: <http://www.linkedin.com/static?key=what_is_linkedin> [Retrieved 12 October 2013].

List 2015. Available at: <http://en.wikipedia.org/wiki/List_of_speech_recognition_software> [Retrieved 29 April 2015].

Maglajlic, S. and Helic, D., 2012. How do social networks influence learning outcomes? A case study in an industrial setting. *Interactive Technology and Smart Education* 9(2), pp. 74–88.

Malamed, C. 2015. Available at: <http://theelearningcoach.com/media/tools-for-interviewing-smes/> [Retrieved 24 April 2015].

NaturallySpeaking 2015. Available at: <www.naturallyspeaking.com> [Retrieved 29 April 2015].

Noffsinger 2015. Available at: <http://www.aapl.org/docs/newsletter/N232voice-recog.htm> [Retrieved 29 April 2015].

Pauleen, D.J., 2003. Leadership in a global virtual team: An action learning approach. *Leadership & Organization Development Journal* 24(3), pp. 153–162.

Plack, M.M., Driscoll. M., Marquez, M. and Greenberg, L., 2010. Peer-facilitated virtual action learning: reflecting on critical incidents during a pediatric clerkship. Available at: <http://www.ncbi.nlm.nih.gov/pubmed/20206914> [Retrieved 12 October 2013].

Rungtusanatham, M., Ellram, L., Siferd, S. and Salik, S., 2004. Toward a typology of business education in the Internet age. *Decision Sciences Journal of Innovative Education* 2(2), pp. 101–120.

Schratz, A., 2014. Available at: <http://www.businessreviewaustralia.com/technology/1073/Interviewing-Goes-Digital> [Retrieved 10 December 2014].

ScreenCastle 2015. Available at: <https://chrome.google.com/webstore/detail/screencastle/anlacahaipmkiacbibndkpkocgocgefb> [Retrieved 24 April 2015].

ScreenFlow 2015. Available at: <http://www.macworld.com/article/2852326/screenflow-5-review-the-macs-best-screencasting-app-gets-better-with-ios-capture.html> [Retrieved 24 April 2015].

Smith, P.A.C. and Coakes, E., 2007. Gaining the competitive edge: Communities of Innovation. *Sociedad & Conocmiento* 4(7), pp. 8–10.

Smith, P.A.C. and Cockburn, T., 2013. *Dynamic Leadership Models for Global Business: Enhancing Digitally Connected Environments*. Hershey, PA: IGI Global.

Smith, P.A.C. and Cockburn, T., (eds). 2014. *The Impact of Emerging Digital Technologies on Leadership in Global Business Environments*. Hershey, PA: IGI Global.

Smith, P.A. and Levinson, S.L., 1996. Business simulations are not just for finance. *Organizations & People* 3(3)., V, No. 3, 1996.

Snow 2015. Available at: <http://www.snow.idrc.ocad.ca/content/voice-recognition-speech-text-software> [Retrieved 29 April 2015].

Snowden, D., 1999. Story telling for the capture and communication of tacit knowledge. Thesis, Indiana University, Bloomington, IN.

Survey 2014. Available at: <http://www.ncbi.nlm.nih.gov/pmc/articles/PMC3124654/> [Retrieved 9 October 2014].

Tosey, P. and Smith, P.A.C., 1999. Assessing the learning organization – Part 2: Exploring practical assessment approaches. *The Learning Organization* 6(3), pp. 107–115.

Total Recorder 2015. Available at: <http://download.cnet.com/Total-Recorder-Standard-Edition/3000-2170_4-10024762.html> [Retrieved 24 April 2015].

Venkatesh 2015. Available at: <http://www.concordia.ca/cunews/main/stories/2012/07/11/new-e-learning-fellow-looks-to-the-future.html> [Retrieved 29 April 2015].

Waddill, D., 2006. Action E-Learning: The impact of action learning on a management-level online course. *Human Resource Development International* 9(2), pp. 1–15.

Wave 2014. Available at: <http://www.theguardian.com/technology/askjack/2008/dec/04/edirol-digital-recorder> [Retrieved 10 December 2014].

Webconfrev 2015. Available at: <http://web-conferencing-services.toptenreviews.com/> [Retrieved 24 April 2015].

Wenger, W., 2000. Communities of practice and social learning systems. Available at: <http://www.linkedin.com/static?key=what_is_linkedin> [Retrieved 14 October 2013].

Wenger, E., 2001. Supporting communities of practice. Available at: <http://www.cin.ufpe.br/~ccte/intranet/01_03_CP_technology_survey_v3.pdf> [Retrieved 1 December 2011].

Wenger, E., McDermott, R. and Snyder, W.M., 2002. *Cultivating Communities of Practice*. Cambridge, MA: Harvard Business School Press.

Zhang, D. 2003. Powering E-learning in the new millennium: An overview of E-learning and enabling technology. *Information Systems Frontiers* 5(2), pp. 201–212.

Chapter 9
Future research impact

Forecasting the future of teams and businesses in an environment of global social and technological complexity is always a precarious business and more so the further ahead we try to envisage their impact. Disruptive changes in technology are complex and seep across and through human society and culture in often-unexpected ways. So some imaginative projection and analysis are required for longer-term views to be more than highly speculative. We don't have jet cars or hovercraft as some speculated. We do have the worldwide web, online banking social media, free video calls and the 'Internet of things' alongside a '24/7' 'always on' culture increasingly spreading across global demographic and geographic domains.

> *Postindustrial enterprises run on intangible assets, such as information, research, development, brand equity, capacity for innovation, and human resources. Yet none of these intangible assets appear on a balance sheet. This is another way of saying that, according to today's accounting practices, the worth of a brand name like Citibank or Ford has no value.*
> (Low and Kalafut, 2002, p. 97)

Equally, as we suggested in earlier chapters, emergence teams may operate across levels from individual to organizational and we need more clarity in our use of terms such as efficiency and effectiveness in teams. As noted by others:

> *Team effectiveness should be more accurately conceptualized as embedded in a multilevel system that has individual, team, and organizational-level aspects; which focuses centrally on task-relevant processes; which incorporates temporal dynamics encompassing episodic tasks and developmental progression; and which views team processes and effectiveness as emergent phenomena unfolding in a ... larger organization system or environmental context.*
> (Kozlowski and Ilgen, 2006, p. 80)

Burtscher and Manser (2012, p. 1344) state that, 'The importance of team mental models (TMMs) – team members' shared and organized understanding of relevant knowledge – for teamwork and team-performance, particularly in high-risk industries, has been recognized for almost two decades.' More specifically, global teams' embedding contexts vary at each of these levels of effectiveness too and thus shared values, usually seen as underpinning trust and actions of teams, varies across cultures. As Nielsen et al. have commented (2007) team contexts are complex and multifaceted and thus far have proved hard to capture in neat definitions or metrics.

In the next decade there will be massive power shift in corporations, with over 50 per cent of Fortune 500 CEOs coming from outside of the EU and USA. Added to that there are demographic changes bubbling up across businesses globally as we indicated (Smith and Cockburn, 2013). As Dan Schawbel (2013) stated in a *Forbes* article, 'By 2025, millennials will account for 75% of the global workforce and by next year, they will account for 36% of the American workforce. At some companies like Accenture and Ernst & Young, they already account for over two thirds of the entire employee base.'

As globalization proceeds and virtual teaming increases, then issues of culture and diversity come to the fore as priorities. Ensuring communication and cultural 'safety' mean more than simply translating instructions from one language to another, so leaders may have to upskill to enter, recruit and manage staff drawn from the global market for talent rather than local labour markets. Such factors as verbal and non-verbal interpretations and understanding, interpersonal behaviour styles, for greetings and discussions between colleagues or co-workers, cultural expectations relating to how other work activities or meetings should proceed or deal with agenda items. For instance, some Pacific island cultures are very religious and expect Christian prayers to be said at the beginning and end of the day, during meetings and ceremonies. Farewells and welcoming or inductions have to be carried out in specific protocol forms according to status and genders present. All of that may conflict with other cultures, especially mainstream western European or US business cultures.

Negotiating styles and individuals' sense of justice or fairness is culturally based (Lewicki et al., 1992, 2003). Thus what is acceptable to ask others to do on certain occasions or with respect to particular tasks or activities is variable. For some Asian cultures saying 'no' directly is regarded as rude behaviour, so a rejection of an offer may necessitate a more roundabout form of expression to avoid causing the other person to lose face and take offence. In a team setting including virtual teams such factors may be more rather than less pronounced.

Consequently teams' shared mental models vary as regards to what is achievable and what are constraints. Conceptually and practically models of how teams function need to attend to the cultural variations as Weir and Hutchings indicated with reference to Nonaka's SECI model (2005). These authors studied how well the model translated into Arab and Chinese cultures and found only partial alignment.

The aspirations and implications of human-machine efficiency and 'algorithmic governance' (technology-controlled systems to ensure law abiding behaviour of citizens such as devices and systems to remotely control automobile speeds on motorways) has been raised in the past but as we get nearer to 'intelligent' robots some research has been initiated into the dynamics of such teams (Schuster et al., 2011, Cockburn et al., 2015). As might be expected, governments and the military are active in this field with research on ways to reduce human troop injuries and fatalities, for example by substituting machines or drones, for fighting, spying, bomb disposal and so on. Such work may have spin-off benefits for civilians too in much the same way as military medicine has significantly impacted on wound treatments, plastic surgery techniques and so on. There are also active research projects in diverse areas such as medicine, counselling, prosthetics, social care, policing, various smart appliances, risk evaluation and many others.

There are, too, growing public interest areas of concern about actual or potential moral panics and ethical dilemmas or problems in need of resolution to protect citizens from panoptic surveillance and infringement of civil liberties, subtly emergent 'censorship' and gatekeeping processes in Wikipedia and social media as well as from cyber thieves, hackers, assorted technical 'glitches' of accidental downloads of personal information, 'accidental' cascades of shares sold by algorithmic systems in foreign currency exchanges or deliberate manipulations of stock exchange posts (Müller-Birn et al., 2013; Chaboud et al., 2014; Smith and Cockburn, 2013, 2014; Cockburn et al., 2015; Napoli, 2015).

There have been many fictional versions of artificial intelligence (AI) or human–computer and human–robot interactions as well as prognostications and cogitations by experts such as Turing (1950) on the character and processes involved in building and using 'thinking machines'. The fictional narratives range from the dystopian to the utopian, often reflecting current issues, threats, assumed potential remedies improvements or concerns occupying many people at the time they were written. Narratives such as Fritz Lang's in his 1927 film, 'Metropolis', 'Artificial Intelligence' (2001), I, robot (2004), Robot and Frank (2012) and so on, on the one hand, through comedic versions such as the factory worker in Charlie Chaplin's 'modern times' have sub texts of alienation, fears, phobias and assumptions about the tyrannical nature of such 'progress' on people and society. Many such fictional accounts have triggered the imagination and enthusiasm of scientists and engineers from early space exploration researchers at NASA, IT design and manufacturing pioneers such as Turing, Watson, Wozniak, Gates, Jobs and so on, through to surgeons and social engineers of various types. Many of the previous worries or hopes may now seem forlorn, misplaced, misdirected or exaggerated to current audiences or readers. Other worries such as surveillance remain, especially by secret government agencies of the 'big brother' type as has been portrayed in the leaked documents of former intelligence service whistleblower Edward Snowden.

Conversational flows in liminal spaces

Teleworking can result in significant cost savings and reduce firms' real estate footprint. As populations increase and so too does longevity, the complexity of healthcare requires increased need for teamwork and interdisciplinary coordination in order to maintain a safe and effective patient treatment (Burtscher and Manser, 2012). However, there are some concerns regarding the optimum technology to sustain virtual teaming and relevant factors such as interrelationships within the team, between the team and others, identification with the group and commitment (or other kinds of orientations) to group and goals. 'Unified communications' capabilities such as voice, chat, and web and video conferencing stretching across desktop and mobile devices are being further developed with linked intelligent interaction and search/retrieve capabilities to better facilitate collaborative activity.

E-mail is old hat and a bit clunky these days and limits what may be discerned about some of the factors listed. Instant messages may be OK as alerts but limited for discussion of any depth and social chat pages can get cluttered very quickly and thus reduce focus or increase search times. People seek streamlined tools to enable catch ups in real time and reduce file management requirements as well as encouraging collaborative work practices such as editing/preparing reports moving beyond basic Wiki technology or systems such as Google Plus.

Socio-digital technology applications have made a global reach within the sights of many SMEs today. Even small start-ups can aim to market goods and services online and so reach suppliers, markets and consumers across the globe. In addition, there is a new generation of digital natives used to the media and who expect it to form a major part of their life such that it begins to function and seem akin to utilities such as electricity or water and thereby is also increasingly 'invisible' (Smith and Cockburn, 2014).

In parallel with the rise of social media tools, some silos and boundaries are breaking down. For example, unified communications including big data has enabled customers and consumers to become a key part of teams, both explicitly with feedback but also tacitly via data gathering from cookies, competitions and conversations of various kinds to establish current consumption patterns or future trends modelling in savvy organizations. This allows links to be made between some people and some organizations who would not normally connect or who connect better now in some new and creative ways forming 'brand communities', and amplifying conversational flows around specific ideas, commodities and issues.

In the course of reaching out they may form temporary or permanent alliances or mobile delivery systems or franchise their branded goods, services and systems to others. Those others may in turn also initiate a series of such with teams of temporary, casual or permanent core and periphery staff and supervision at a distance as virtual teaming increases. In 2013, the US Association for Talent Development cited a study conducted by Nemertes Research company, showing that virtual workers in the US had increased 800 per cent in the five years from 2008 (Dennis et al., 2013). Online services reduce the costs and size of in-house IT servicing, so companies are moving systems onto the cloud where the managed services providers do the work. Teaming is part of the foundational ideas of cloud-based systems thus emergence teams may be operated in a similar virtualized manner.

One aspect of the rise of virtual teaming in many industries and sectors is that remote working doesn't always currently fit the brand, the goods or the services that every company or organization produces. Thus there is a flux in the relationships across the business, profession, industry or markets of many organizations but not all of them as yet. For instance, some luxury goods have consumers who insist on personal service and being able to see products, some other services require 'hands on' service such as invasive medical treatments and care, though some health testing might be carried out remotely.

For example, a number of years ago, one of the current authors (Cockburn) undertook research on a pilot project on remote aftercare services for cardiac patients in the UK. The organization concerned provided a service enabling patients to have their heart rate and/or treatment progress monitored remotely. The process involved using a credit card-like device and an ordinary phone line linked to trained technicians who recorded the data from the device. Thus medical teams were able to analyse and discuss such data or to advise patients if an urgent visit was needed.

Although there are some 'technical', service or customer-related reasons for certain companies deciding virtual teaming is inappropriate, in part, this reluctance also relates to the levels of trust between management and staff. As we discussed in earlier chapters, the processes of building or putting together an emergence team necessitates high trust and high commitment expectations as foundations for greater confidence, team efficacy, as well as cognitive agility and emotional resilience in the face of challenge and thereby less chance of groupthink. Changing over to online teaming may be executed incrementally and aligned with social changes as more and more people use and expect an 'app' for everything. As has been recently pointed out:

> *The telephone took 76 years to reach half of all US households. The Smartphone reached the same level of penetration in less than a decade.*
>
> (PWC, 2014, p. 12)

Automation and robotics applications for emergence teaming?

Could we have robot teams to replace people anytime soon? That seems unlikely in the next decade or so given the current costs of producing them and the limitations they still appear to have. Factory automation and robot use is not yet standard practice and varies according to the nature of the product. Thus, true to the spirit of F.W. Taylor's principles on 'scientific' management', car producers have automated four-fifths of their assembly processes whereas electronics is only 10 per cent automated, due to the more frequent changes or customization required in the processes as people change or upgrade products such as cellphones more often than cars (Rus, 2015). If we were being somewhat more sceptical we might also remark upon the reduced labour costs from offshoring production as a trade-off factor in the lower levels of automation in some manufacturing too.

However, although there is an emerging trend to apply digital technology and crowd sourcing to some professional jobs as we noted elsewhere (Smith and Cockburn, 2013), the use of emergence teams is of a different order from assembly line production and routine professional roles too. Many experts in automation, business and robotics are agreed that humans retain higher cognitive and creative agility in many areas to date and we still prefer human-to-human interaction in many service areas (Gratton, 2015a). Thus, it is more likely that automation and robots will be applied to augment or complement teams in the short term or policy preferences for retaining wholly or partly human staff in some areas may be proposed to slow down or limit further automation (Brynjolfsson and McAfee, 2015; Rus 2015). We should also be wary of some of the currently perceived benefits since social attitudes change with rising generations and their expectations and education. Online professional and social networks often seem to simulate what's happening offline though sometimes with higher visibility and acceleration of incipient changes becoming realized as the 'new normal' – at least 'pro tem'.

An example of that may be seen in the medical sphere. A number of years ago some research was conducted in the UK to evaluate the application of automation to medical counselling for sexually transmitted illnesses. It was regarded as a means of avoiding patient embarrassment about discussing the topic with their local doctor in a surgery. The experiment was found to have some perceived benefits for some such patients at the time but since then social mores have changed, in part as a result of television programmes on topics relating to medicine and the popularity of programmes on pregnancy, plastic surgery and more specifically 'didactic' ones such as 'Embarrassing Bodies' which discusses embarrassing ailments and their treatment. So, in the UK now, more people are willing to step forward and discuss matters they previously saw as stigmatizing or undiscussable in 'polite company'.

Rewards for future teams?

According to a *Fortune* magazine online article, AI will mean that up to 50 per cent of what knowledge workers do now will be done by machines, not simply because it will be done more speedily but also because humans have biases, skewing decision making and actions (Fisher 2014). 'The upside: AI will free up human talent for more interesting, creative work' according to Fisher's expert interviewee. The latter speculation about potential human gains is a topic taken up by others.

From a slightly different perspective it is proposed that a factor that will influence future teams of people (as opposed to AI machines) is the rewards system and, within that, the type and amount of rewards sought and achieved. Typically, many people simply regard rewards as tangible in the form of money. However, HR researcher Professor Lynda Gratton (2015b), commenting in her blog, has suggested that intangible rewards will be the ones that work best in future, especially for those in ageing societies such as the USA, the EU and Japan where more people are living longer. Living to be 100 is not unimaginable and there are increasing numbers of centenarians in the more affluent societies today. Those older workers, she suggests, will seek more than money from working into their 80s and beyond. They will be searching for:

> *Work that is valuable both now and as a hedge against the future has three crucial elements:*
>
> *It is interesting and allows workers to engage their mind and creativity*
>
> *It has developmental potential – particularly to in terms of capabilities that are 'portable' in the sense that they can be used beyond the current job*
>
> *It is non-routine so is unlikely to be substituted in the short term by robotics or Artificial Intelligence.*
>
> *(Gratton, 2015b)*

She also sees such a trend as likely to have ripple effects elsewhere in businesses; raising the value of some employees relative to others and altering the way work and remuneration are calculated. If accurate, this sort of motivated staff and rewards system should positively benefit emergence teams given features we have already discussed in earlier chapters.

References

Brynjolfsson, E. and Andrew McAfee., 2015. Will humans go the way of horses? Labor in the second machine age *Foreign Affairs*. Available at: <https://www.foreignaffairs.com/articles/2015-06-16/will-humans-go-way-horses> [Accessed 19 June 2015].

Burtscher, M.J. and Manser, T., 2012. Team mental models and their potential to improve teamwork and safety: A review and implications for future research in healthcare. *Safety Science* 50, pp. 1344–1354.

Chaboud, A.P., Chiquoine, B., Hjalmarsson, E. and Vega, C., 2014. Rise of the machines: Algorithmic trading in the Foreign Exchange Market. *The Journal of Finance* 69(5), pp. 2045–2084.

Cockburn, T., Jahdi, K. and Wilson, E. (eds), 2015. *Responsible Governance: International Perspectives for the New Era*. New York, NY: Business Expert Press.

Denis, D., Meola, D and Hall, M.J., 2013. *Effective Leadership in a Virtual Workforce*. Association for Talent Development. Available at: <https://www.

td.org/Publications/Magazines/TD/TD-Archive/2013/02/Effective-Leadership-in-a-Virtual-Workforce> [Accessed 18 August 2015].

Fisher, A., 2014. 3 workplace trends to watch for in 2015 (and beyond). *Fortune (online)*. Available at: <http://fortune.com/2014/12/04/workplace-office-future-predictions/> [Accessed 18 June 2015].

Gratton, L., 2015a. What will artificial intelligence do for work? January 22, blog. Available at: <http://lyndagrattonfutureofwork.typepad.com> [Accessed 18 June 2015].

Gratton, L., 2015b. What if money was no longer the most valuable asset a company could offer an employee? June 1, blog. Available at: <http://lyndagrattonfutureofwork.typepad.com> [Accessed 19 June 2015].

Kozlowski, S.W.J. and Ilgen, D.R., 2006. Enhancing the effectiveness of work groups and teams. *Psychological Science in the Public Interest* 7(3). pp. 77–124.

Lewicki, R.J., Barry, B., Saunders, D.M. and Minton, J.W., 2003. *Negotiation* (4th Ed.). Boston, MA: McGraw-Hill Higher Education.

Lewicki, R.J., Weiss, S.E. and Lewin, D., 1992. Models of conflict, negotiation and third party intervention: a review and synthesis. *Journal of Organizational Behavior* 13(3), pp. 209–252.

Low, J. and Kalafut, P.C., 2002. *Invisible Advantage: How Intangibles are Driving Business Performance*. Cambridge, MA: Perseus Publishing.

Müller-Birn, C., Dobusch, L. and Herbsleb, J.D., 2013. Work-to-rule: the emergence of algorithmic governance in Wikipedia. *Proceedings of the 6th International Conference on Communities and Technologies*, New York, NY: ACT, pp. 80–89.

Napoli, P.M., 2015. Social media and the public interest: Governance of news platforms in the realm of individual and algorithmic gatekeepers. *Telecommunications Policy*. In Press, Corrected Proof, accessed, June 2015.

Nielsen, T.M., Edmondson, A.C. and Sundstrom, E., 2007. Team wisdom: Definition, dynamics, and applications. In Kessler, E. and Bailey, J. eds. *Handbook of Organizational and Managerial Wisdom*, pp. 21–42. Thousand Oaks, CA: Sage.

PWC 2014. Fit for the future-Capitalising on global trends, Price Waterhouse Cooper. Available at: <http://www.pwc.com/ceosurvey> [Accessed 30 June 2014].

Rus, D., 2015. The robots are coming. How technological breakthroughs will transform everyday life. *Foreign Affairs*. Available at: <https://www.foreignaffairs.com/articles/2015-06-16/robots-are-coming> [Accessed 19 June 2015].

Schawbel, D., 2013. 10 ways millennials are creating the future of work. *Forbes*. Available at: <http://onforb.es/18QL7p3> [Accessed 11 June 2015].

Schuster, D., Ososky, S., Jentsch, F., Phillips, E., Lebiere, C., & Evans, A.W. 2011. A Research Approach to Shared Mental Models and Situation Assessment in

Future Robot Teams. Proceedings of the Human Factors and Ergonomics Society Annual Meeting. Santa Monica, CA: Human Factors and Ergonomics Society.

Smith, P. and Cockburn, T., 2013. *Dynamic Leadership Models for Global Business: Enhancing Digitally Connected Environments*. Hershy, PA: IGI Global.

Smith, P. and Cockburn, T., eds, 2014. *Impact of Emerging Digital Technologies on Leadership in Global Business*. Hershy, PA: IGI Global.

Turing, A.M., 1950. Computing Machinery and Intelligence. *Mind* 59(236), pp. 433–460.

Weir, D. and Hutchings, K., 2005. Cultural embeddedness and contextual constraints: Knowledge sharing in Chinese and Arab cultures. *Knowledge and Process Management* 12(2), pp. 89–98.

Chapter 10
Revised case study

Ineffective leadership

The notion of organizational leadership has traditionally been viewed in a top-down reductionist way of thinking at Nordica TV. At the pinnacle of the organization it has been the preserve of the CEO, followed by the other C-suite incumbents, then senior executives, then middle management and so on throughout the hierarchy. The idea that an organization's board of directors has the ultimate leadership responsibility has never been considered since the company had traditionally operated very profitably, and the role of a CEO had become so dominant that no chairman wanted to fight a leadership battle with so little business ammunition in hand. However, as noted elsewhere:

> Today the Boards of listed companies in developed countries are generally also seen as a mechanism for ensuring accurate risk intelligence, for directing the company effectively and sustainably whilst monitoring the agency costs of executive and operational management systems. This involves a notional IOU regarding the future. The future, however, is inherently and increasingly uncertain or ambiguous, hence the nature and value of any future claim is also uncertain. That is, it is contingent on events that have yet to occur.
> (Cockburn et al., 2015, p. 2)

The company has had dwindling audiences for its scheduled programmes over the last few years due to the rise in consumers using Internet TV, and the board of directors has finally realized that 'Business as usual' was untenable in their current VUCA business environment, particularly given that the in-company initiatives detailed in the Test Case in Chapter 1 were clearly ineffective and bankruptcy was staring them in the face. In principle, the board of directors was ideally placed to envisage and lead the demanding journey back to profitability and employee security, given that it had responsibility for the interests of all the stakeholders, not just shareholders, as its mandate.

Without the board of directors' interest, broad experience, vision, knowledge and leadership, regarding a chosen sustainable business variant, it was not likely that anyone else in the organization would pay much attention to the company's problems, other than with some 'window dressing', and this attitude had been borne out through the initiatives detailed in the Test Case in Chapter 1. This is a serious concern, since if the board of directors does not understand the essence of the organizational change necessary, the risk is that top management will be replaced with new managers who have new ideas of their own. Organizations are replete with change credibility 'black holes' created when change sponsors have moved on from their much-hyped initiatives without accomplishing their objectives.

Given the lacklustre results reported in the Test Case detailed in Chapter 1, Nordica's chairman and a number of influential members of the board felt that 'enough was enough', and they met together to map out a new strategy. The chairman and a number of these board members were familiar with the research and recommendations of Smith and Cockburn (2013, 2014; this volume, 2016) in regard to leadership capabilities, and their recent recommendations concerning emergence teams and the capability such an approach would offer to address the kind of problem Nordica was facing. With strong board member backing, the chairman 'influenced' the CEO to adopt the emergence team process detailed by Smith and Cockburn (this volume, 2016), and the senior organizational management committee (including the C-suite) were fully briefed on what this approach would entail, and the penalties of not fully supporting it.

Introducing the emergence team initiative

Although Nordica's CEO had not initially been conversant with the emergence team process, she quickly grasped its promise and realized that by adopting it wholeheartedly she could regain her leadership influence at the board level. With the CEO 'onside', the management team and C-suite members also enthusiastically began to plan how to implement the emergence team process. The first step involved supplying all members of the management team with copies of Smith and Cockburn (this volume, 2016) so that they would all be conversant with the emergence team process. This was followed by a number of detailed meetings between the CEO, management team members, Peter Smith and Dr Tom Cockburn, to familiarize management in detail with the process steps, and their responsibilities in the process. In the past, a chief knowledge management officer (CKMO) had been identified, and although his role had become diminished, it was decided that this individual should assume the title of chief emergence team officer (CETO) with responsibility for sponsoring the emergence team initiative, and for coordinating cross-organizational efforts.

The CETO immediately arranged to meet with Nordica's IT management to explore development and activation of a crowdsourcing system. Some years previously, Nordica had successfully introduced a company-wide statistical quality control programme and the CETO consulted with the head of this programme to better understand details of how it was successfully rolled out. On the basis of this advice the CETO scheduled a number of information sessions across the organization where Peter Smith and Dr Tom Cockburn could lead the audience through the process steps in appropriate detail and answer questions. Successful uptake had been demonstrated in the past for Nordica's statistical quality control programme using this approach, where the key speaker at these sessions had been W.A. Shewhart. In the role of the emergence team's sponsor the CETO developed an emergence team role statement (see Example 2.1 in Chapter 2 for a template) and worked with management team members to reach consensus on the individual elements of this statement. The only area of disagreement centred on how the emergence team would be rewarded for a successful team effort. Finally it was decided to reward the whole team rather than individual members and the reward would involve additional holiday time for each team member.

Rolling out the crowdsourcing effort

At this point, Nordica's employees had digested the announcement regarding the emergence team approach, and had explored its implications among themselves and with opinion leaders across the organization. There was widespread appreciation of the opportunity to contribute to solving Nordica's problem via the crowdsourcing method rather than via the traditional Nordica top-down approach, and enthusiasm was high to make the intervention a success. At this point the CETO (with the IT department's blessing) thought it appropriate to roll out the crowdsourcing initiative. Response was strong and the CETO's staff compiled lists (from the crowdsourcing responses) of recommended team members, team leaders and individuals as potential storytellers.

Identification of team leader and choosing team members

The CETO next arranged interviews with the potential team leaders identified. The choice for team leader was greatly facilitated when one of the nominated candidates proved to have considerable previous experience in team management, although not with emergence teams. A preliminary list of chosen potential team leaders was presented by the CETO at a special management meeting, and based on a recommendation by the CETO and consensus with the other senior managers and the CEO, the choice was narrowed down to the one experienced individual.

After a further interview with the CETO this individual was chosen as the formal emergence team leader, and the CEO and the CETO then jointly announced to the organization the name of the new team leader. The CETO and the team leader now held a series of interviews with potential team members to finalize the team make-up. Nordica's manufacturing and headquarters facilities are all situated in the same city, which facilitated team members meeting together in person. Team members chosen were advised of their team inclusion, and an announcement was circulated across the organization identifying these individuals; appropriate arrangements were also made across the organization to release these individuals for team duty. Copies of Smith and Cockburn (this volume, 2016) were provided to the team leader and team members for reference purposes.

The foundation and leadership process that Smith and Cockburn (2013, pp. 39–55) describe provides a process that takes into account the existing knowledge of the team leader and provides a framework to further expand this knowledge, or as appropriate, to 'unlearn' previously developed knowledge and skills that the individual now finds counterproductive. This is a process of continuous optimization and adaptation, where the next leadership action is based on what is happening 'now'. In other words, team leadership is emergent, and is co-developed and aligned with the context in which the team activity leadership is taking place. Smith and Cockburn (2013, p. 39) assert that, 'Now and in the future leadership is all about having a vision with an uncertain path to its achievement that may only be navigated through flexibility, agility, learning and unlearning, based on the leader's own knowledge and experience, and the collaborative wisdom of fellow stakeholders.'

Team leader activities

The first step for the team leader in the process recommended by Smith and Cockburn (2013, pp. 40–54) involved the team leader having excellent clarity and understanding of his leadership role – in essence, what the team leader and the team were expected to achieve. The role defined by the team sponsor (the CETO) was carefully studied by the team leader and was then finalized and refined through further careful clarification and consultation between the team leader and the CETO. Written documentation of their agreement was produced thereafter.

The next step involved the team leader analysing how to successfully perform his role. This was accomplished using the performance system model presented in Figure 4.1 in Chapter 4. The team leader felt that he had a clear Focus on what his role demanded, and that his Will to succeed was very strong; however he felt that under Capability his lack of experience in action learning and dialogue needed to be addressed before the full team process began. The team leader explored these issues with the CETO, and it was decided that an experienced action learning Set adviser consultant would be contracted to support the team leader as he carried out his 'emcee' action learning role with the team. To address another Capability shortfall, the team leader and the CETO booked a 'permanent' meeting room for the emergence team's use.

Team meetings

At this point the team leader initiated the first team meeting. Arranging this meeting was greatly simplified since all team members were located within short distances of one another. The team leader and team members quickly reached consensus on 'How will ongoing decisions be made?' and then explored their understanding of, and readiness to undertake, the consensus process. The team leader and the team then developed a simple set of team meeting ground rules. These rules were written on a large flip chart and posted prominently on the meeting room wall.

After these opening steps the team leader presented to team members a copy of the written and 'confirmed' team sponsor/team leader questionnaire (see Chapter 2); time was then allowed for team members to digest this document and discuss it among themselves in a later private team member session. Questions or concerns arising from this discussion were highlighted with the team leader at a follow-up meeting where all issues raised were quickly resolved. The team decided that a further meeting with the team sponsor did not appear warranted.

Next, the team leader staged a brainstorming/knowledge sharing session to facilitate creative knowledge exchange and sensemaking among all the team members with regard to Nordica's problem and the challenges that the team faced. The team then held a meeting at which they drafted a statement of team purpose and identified potential barriers that they perceived. The major barrier identified was the length of time it would take the team to conduct appropriate interviews across the organization, document the interviews and draw conclusions. The team leader was requested to highlight this concern with the CETO and management team. At their next meeting team members agreed on a metaphor that described the kind of team that team members envisaged they needed to form. They opted for visualizing themselves as a team of investigative journalists.

At the next meeting the team decided on the manner in which information would be captured, documented and shared among team members. The team leader also set up meetings with vendors of audio/visual equipment to assess the kinds of equipment the team would need for the interviewing phases of their work, and appropriate equipment was purchased for them by the CETO. With the team leader's guidance, team members then organized a series of interview training sessions for themselves which entailed each team member interviewing (using the new audio/visual equipment) another team member in the presence of the team group followed by group members and the interviewee then providing feedback to the interviewer. In this way, all team members gained considerable learning and experience both with the interview process and the audio/visual equipment.

During the above period, the team leader together with the action learning consultant had also organized a series of action learning sessions where each team member presented to the team an organizational problem which they had been facing in real life. Team members then practised addressing the particular problem using the action learning process. This included recommending an action step that would have been undertaken in a real-life action learning situation. Emphasis in these sessions was placed on the processes of reflection and dialogue as well the action learning process itself.

The interview phase

At this point pressure was mounting in the senior management ranks to see some results from the emergent team initiative, and the team leader also felt that the team was ready to move into the Norming and Performing stages of their team activity. The team leader recommended to the team members that they begin to arrange and carry out interviews with the nominated storytellers across the organization, and team members began to engage in iterative cycles of information collection and storage and sensemaking. To the extent possible, information and sources were checked for validity, and a preliminary story draft was prepared.

Using this story draft, and subsequent redrafts, team sessions using the Performance Learning process described in Chapter 6 were held. The team employed the process used in the approach illustrated in Figure 6.1 in Chapter 6 to assess the problem environment that Nordica faced. The team assessed Nordic's problem situation as 'complex' since the problem story they had drafted demonstrated very poor organizational understanding of the problem (poor Focus); seemingly little or no new relevant technological expertise (poor Capability); and due to the cycles of enthusiasm and disappointment when seemingly appropriate action had failed or had produced unexpected second tier problems, with the organization sinking deeper into a pit of uncertainty and despair (poor Will).

Problem definition and follow-up action

The role statement had not suggested that the emergence team actually undertake any actions to resolve the Nordica problem, but had indicated that a clear definition of the problem would count as success, together with recommendations for next steps. The team recommended that the steps listed in Chapter 1, and described by Snowden and Boone (2007, p. 73) for dealing with complex environments, be applied in going forward organizationally:

1. 'Open up the discussion, more interaction is required than in any other context

2. Set barriers to delineate behavior

3. Stimulate attractors – probes that resonate with people

4. Encourage dissent and diversity

5. Focus on creating an environment within which good things may emerge rather than trying to bring about predetermined results.'

The emergence team further explored, described and recommended this approach to its sponsor as an 'Adaptive Strategy' where Nordica's outdated classical strategy would in future be based on practice rather than on analysis and design. To accomplish this, the company must become more 'agile' so that it could respond quickly to market changes. The traditional Nordica 'looking backwards' approach to its business must change to one where players would think through all of the alternatives, and identify and prepare contingency plans to withstand the inevitable surprises. Innovation and experimentation must become the organization's normal business practice where the most promising variations and innovations would be further tested through pilot projects conducted directly in the marketplace. Continuous fine-tuning in all aspects of the organization would become the 'new norm'. The team also recommended that action learning be adopted across the organization both to develop adaptive leaders and as a means of addressing problems in an inclusive manner. The team recommended that this process be termed 'action adaption' to emphasize its innovative organizational focus; and that the process must include reflection using the Performance Model (Focus, Will and Capability) that the team had utilized. The team also highlighted the success other large traditional organizations had achieved in becoming more agile and customer-driven using this performance approach (Smith and Saint-Onge, 1996; Smith, 2007).

The team's sponsor supported the team's proposals and presented them to the C-suite and the board. After detailed discussion and further team presentations, the team's recommendations were accepted and implemented successfully with beneficial business results for Nordica.

Using the above approach, the emergence team resolved the major organizational problems, some of which were identified in Chapter 1 and which are summarized below:

- inability to grasp new business opportunities;
- ineffective leadership;
- incomplete exploration of the problem situation;
- limited motivation and focus on project priority tasks;
- insufficient team member skills and capabilities for the project;
- lack of collaboration and teamwork;
- unclear goals and objectives;
- conscripted rather than selected or volunteered membership.

The ongoing legacy of the emergence team initiative

The new CETO, emergence team and project review process is central to demonstrating leadership, probing more deeply into ongoing and emergent issues and problems. Culture can affect how your employees react to changes. The processes involved in so doing also contribute to building a new story for the company, and driving staff motivation as a vehicle which provides an opportunity for all to participate and be consulted. This is true at board and C-suite levels as Nordica's experience demonstrated.

Research has indicated that individuals in workplaces adopt nuanced and differentiated orientations towards various other actors, systems, processes and actions. People can adopt a multi-foci perspective distinguishing between perceived fairness or levels of 'justice' they see exhibited between these foci. Thus, they are most likely to trust and cooperate freely with systems – whether they themselves win or lose by those systems – when they perceive that a fair process and fair intent as well as open and fair consultation, involvement and reflection has been followed throughout inauguration and execution of the system and subsequent actions (Lavelle et al., 2007). The adverse effects of low trust between employees and management are thereby neutralized and leaders can catalyse the power of the community of practice to enact changes necessary (Kim and Mauborgne, 2003, p. 132). Further, the open and transparent selection procedure for the goals of the project and the selection and recruitment of a team leader and CETO had been exemplary in demonstrating that most well-suited candidates had been considered carefully, selection had been fair and that the further development of the team to meet the tasks set had begun. The latter procedures and outcomes also indicate that commitment to the team and these processes can significantly impact on performance and results. As Lavelle et al. (2007) note:

> *In a team setting, Bishop et al. (2000) found that employee commitment to the team predicted job performance (path estimate = .45), whereas organizational commitment did not. Moreover, team commitment mediated the relationship between team support and job performance, whereas organizational support was not significantly correlated with performance.*
>
> (Lavelle et al., 2007, p. 859)

The last two Nordica engagement surveys prior to the inauguration of the emergence team process had highlighted four critical issues for employees:

1. Lack of clear goal setting.

2. Lack of constructive feedback.

3. Reward strategy not integrated with the review process, and not linking performance with rewards offered.

4. Staff expressing concerns about their future and Nordica's support for them in developing their abilities.

Lack of clear goals and feedback through a properly integrated approach to performance management had been affecting employee satisfaction and development, and hindering alignment of individual performance with objectives of the organization. The organization-wide emergence team information sessions and the inclusive nature of the crowdsourcing exercise, plus the post-emergence team introduction of action adaption, went a long way to erase the impact of the previous traditional Nordica initiatives. Although many researchers have traditionally examined stages or facets of emotional dynamics in isolation from each other, we argue that such aspects (and the resultant emotional regimes in communities, teams and companies) are formed by interconnectedness. Even if working 'solo', staff are inevitably connected to the organizational culture and professional culture as it relates to the organization, incorporating intra-individual, individual, interpersonal and organizational levels of analysis. At the organizational level we need to look at the embedding culture and, specifically, what Schein (2005) describes as cultural 'artifacts', 'beliefs' and underlying 'assumptions' that reinforce these aspects in Nordica TV value chain that were failing.

According to 'Putting The Service-Profit Chain To Work' by Heskett et al. (2008), a company's leadership should be able define their leadership culture based on the following leadership characteristics.

To what extent is the company's leadership:

- Energetic, creative versus stately, conservative?

- Participatory, caring versus removed, elitist?

- Listening, coaching and teaching versus supervising and managing?

- Motivating by mission versus motivating by fear?

- Leading by means of personally demonstrated values versus institutionalized policies?

Leaders naturally have individual traits and styles. But the CEOs of companies that are successfully using the service-profit chain possess all or most of a set of traits that separate them from their merely good competitors. Of course, different styles of leadership are appropriate for various stages in an organization's development. But the messages sent by the successful leaders we have observed stress the importance of careful attention to the needs of customers and employees. These leaders create a culture capable of adapting to the needs of both (Heskett et al., 2008) and Nordica's leaders aspired to this with their post-emergence team initiatives.

There are clear signs of problems with pre-existing Nordica TV corporate culture; especially with the senior management's apparent inability (or unwillingness) to correct the ongoing poor performance storyline. The culture of the company resonated with its prior history of being almost akin to a 'utility' as a state broadcaster, that is, highly regulated in its operational activities, somewhat complacent, slow, not responsive generally but punctuated with periodic spasms of kneejerk reactive panics in the face of perceived imminent change or disaster. It had in many ways proven the distinctive characteristics and behaviours of a national institution as described by Edwards and Rees (2006).

> *Differences and changes in central institutional arrangements and agencies have had significant and quite long-standing consequences for the ways in which firms organize and control work, establish networks, and develop growth strategies.*
>
> (Edwards and Rees, 2006)

These 'long-standing consequences' were evident in the organization before the introduction of the emergence team approach, especially in its myopic and reactive growth strategies, which had not been as strong and focused as it's competition and also in the way the organization poorly managed its people. As a result of all these accumulated and unattended to issues there had been an alienating lack of real, functioning employee engagement systems, worsening business outcomes and declining morale as imminent disaster looms large in the eyes of most of the staff. Although there had been staff engagement surveys, they appeared to have been simply 'lip service' acts as the resultant data were not scrutinized too closely nor were they used to enhance how the departments worked.

To enable what Smith and Sharicz (2013) call 'zones of interaction', the first step has now been taken. That is, the creation of a central core of business concepts and shared social norms (an attractor) to be analysed, refined and used by employee networks at all levels to shape the organization in a dynamic manner. The aim being to start 'creating a socialized environment based on trust, true dialogue, and the lessening of the power struggles . . . '. These steps have been initiated by the CEO and CETO.

These results also imply that developing behavioural norms for the emotional awareness in the team contributed to the development of practicable 'Emotional Intelligence' as well as addressing the other dimensions of their story referred to in Chapter 7. That is:

a)   the information level;

b)   the procedural level;

c)   the emotional level.

So, the leaders are now also focused on constructing a broader, agreed set of norms for the organization's emotional health and well-being regulation and these regulation norms are positively correlated with improved performance. That also influenced the emergence team's decentring approach to their role, reinforcing the climate of safety within this team and between the team and other teams they interacted with internally. Addressing emergence will not be a one-off action as the VUCA context is also evolving, but like 'Red Cross teams in disaster zones, some "bubbles" of safety around core procedures and expert teams can be created' (Oakes and Weissenberg, 2015).

By systematically and iteratively cascading, discussing and agreeing objectives through the action adaption process at both team and individual levels across the organization, current and future performance standards will be clarified and may be consistently applied and reviewed to build a more performance-oriented culture. Everyone within the organization then feels included and also then much more accountable for performance either directly or indirectly. They are also aware of the relevant parts of the business strategy and the implications for their part of the business. All staff members are more inclined towards being proactive in providing new ideas, feedback and suggestions for things to include in action plans to improve the overall performance. By supporting a developmental focus on a combination of capability to deliver and willingness to commit to supporting the strategy, both Nordica TV and its employees are better set to meet the future needs of the market, and expectations from both parties are systematically clarified and reviewed, further establishing a mutual commitment to a unified perspective.

Timeframes plus narrative frames matter

It is a cliché but true, 'Rome wasn't built in a day' and there will be many small successes en route and as the VUCA environment evolves. As Kanter (2013) states:

> *Turnarounds operate on several time frames. There are big strategies and systems that take a long time to shift – think IT, which almost never works the first time, as Americans see in the hasty failed implementation of the Affordable Care Act website. Meanwhile, there are numerous small wins if everyone is engaged. While Verizon worked on shifting the momentum from landlines and voice to smartphones, FiOS (fiber-optic communication systems), and cloud services, mini-innovators created software and streamlined processes.*
> (Kanter, 2013)

The small victories may also be motivators to be communicated across the stakeholder communities to assist in reinforcing the will to change and to provide milestones showing measurable progress. The Nordica TV community is diverse; there are creatives as well as journalists, administrators and executives as well as technicians and ultimately consumers to consider to varying degrees at various points along the timeline of the emergence project and ultimate recovery and turnaround.

The emergence team recommended that a specific survey should also be set up later to measure how the revised knowledge and action adaption systems are operating and how review processes are understood, received and implemented in order to gain insight into elements that may not be working as intended. In summary, while conducting knowledge work, networks of practice within organizations as well as across them may have different memberships and exchange dynamics compared to those of individuals exchanging knowledge. Thus, studies comparing various levels within, across and between networks and their network dynamics both within and across firms as well as those publicly available on the Internet are necessary as the process proceeds and systems evolve. Commitment beyond recurring reorganizations and change of management must be sought at board level (as was initiated at Nordica TV), to ensure investment and the process not being hampered by recurrences of any of the bureaucratic tendencies inherent in the former systems.

References

Cockburn, T., Jahdi, K. and Wilson, E., eds, 2015. *Responsible Governance: International Perspectives for the New Era.* New York, NY: Business Expert Press.

Edwards, T. and Rees, C., 2006. *International Human Resource Management: Globalization, National Systems and Multinational Companies*. Harlow, UK: FT Prentice Hall.

Heskett, J., Jones, T., Loveman, G., Sarrer, E. and Schlesinger, L., 2008. Putting the service-profit chain to work. *Harvard Business Review* 86, pp. 118–129.

Kanter, R.M., 2013. How to turn around nearly anything. *Harvard Business Review*, 5 November. Available at: <https://hbr.org/2013/11/how-to-turn-around-nearly-anything/> [Accessed 19 June 2015].

Kim, W.C. and Mauborgne, R., 2003. Fair process: Managing in the knowledge economy. *Harvard Business Review* 81(1) pp. 127–136.

Lavelle, J.J., Rupp, D.E. and Brockner, J., 2007. Taking a multifoci approach to the study of justice, social exchange, and citizenship behavior: The target similarity model. *Journal of Management* 33(6), pp. 841–866.

Oakes, G. and Weissenberg, M., 2015. Governance and agility in product development organizations. In Cockburn, T., Jahdi, K. and Wilson, E. eds. *Responsible Governance: International Perspectives for the New Era*. New York, NY: Business Expert Press, pp. 39–90.

Schein, E.H., 2005. Taking organization culture seriously. In Rothwell, W.J. and Sullivan. R. eds. *Practicing Organization Development*. San Francisco, CA: Pfeiffer, pp. 365–375.

Smith, P.A.C., 1997. Performance learning. *Management Decision* 35(10), pp. 721–730.

Smith, P.A.C., 2007. Case study: Planning as learning. *Action Learning Research and Practice* 4(1), pp. 77–86.

Smith, P.A.C. and Cockburn, T., 2013. *Dynamic Leadership Models for Global Business: Enhancing Digitally Connected Environments*. Hershey, PA: IGI Global.

Smith, P.A.C. and Cockburn, T., eds. 2014. *Impact of Emerging Digital Technologies on Leadership in Global Business*. Hershey, PA: IGI Global.

Smith, P.A.C. and Cockburn, T., 2016. *Developing and Leading Emergence Teams: A New Approach for Identifying and Resolving Complex Business Problems*. Aldershot, UK: Gower.

Smith, P.A.C. and Saint-Onge, H., 1996. The evolutionary organization: Avoiding a Titanic fate. *The Learning Organization* 3(4), pp. 4–21.

Smith, P.A.C. and Sharicz, C., 2011. The shift needed for sustainability. *The Learning Organization* 18(1), pp. 72–86.

Smith, P.A.C. and Sharicz, C.A., 2013. The bi-modal organization: Balancing autopoiesis and fluid social networks for sustainability. *The Learning Organization* 20(2), pp. 134–152.

Snowden, D.J. and Boone, M.E., 2007. A Leader's Framework for Decision Making. *Harvard Business Review*, November, pp. 1–8.

Acknowledgement

Many people and resources have contributed to our book at various times and in various ways, including leading researchers , practitioners and consultants on whose experiences and insights we have relied in developing our book, and we sincerely thank them all.

In particular we would like to single out some contributors whom we feel merit specific mention. In this regard we wish to gratefully acknowledge Dr. Henk Eijkman for generously offering to write the Foreword. We also thank Prof. Eve Mittleton-Kelly, Dr. Anthony Normore and Dr. Greg Wang for their supportive Endorsements, and David Snowden for generously making available to us the Cynefin framework diagram .

We are also pleased to acknowledge the invaluable help and support provided to us by the Gower and Ashgate editorial staffs in the reviewing, finalizing, publishing, and marketing stages of our book, including Jonathan Norman, Rachel Lynch, Christine Muddiman, Sara Hutton, Emily Pace, and Charlotte Parkins.

Lastly, but by no means less importantly, we enthusiastically thank our spouses Lorraine Smith and Mary Cockburn, for their encouragement, support and unbelievable patience during the researching and writing of this book.

Index

Acephalous 112; *see also* emotional regimes
act (unknowable chaotic) 58; *see also* Cynefin framework
action adaption 157, 159, 161, 162
action learning 6–10, 19, 20, 22, 24, 28, 29, 43, 63–4, 69, 70–2, 76–7, 85, 87–8, 107–10, 123–6, 129, 154–5, 157
affordances 28, 68, 72
algorithmic governance 142
alienation 62, 143
'always on' culture 140
anxiety 58, 69, 73, 78–9, 94, 111–13
archetypal systemic loops 79
artificial intelligence 142, 147
Artisan 45–6, 58–9; *see also* Guardian; Rational
attractors 4, 79, 105–6, 156

behaviour 4, 26, 40, 156; *see also* team behaviours
belief box 110
bifurcation 72, 75
binary social relationship 79
boundaries 6, 19, 26–7, 33, 46, 53, 59, 80, 94, 102, 108, 144
boundary-scanning 109
bounded 104
brainstorming 55, 154

capability 26, 45, 51–3, 72, 76, 78, 80, 88, 89–93, 113, 122–4, 131–2, 134, 151, 154, 156, 157, 161

cast and props 110–11
change credibility 151
Change Proofing 91–2
Chief Emergence Team officer (CETO) 151
Chief Executive Officer (CEO) 17, 20, 33, 35, 141, 150–1, 153, 159, 161
Chief Knowledge Management Officer (CKMO) 151
climate 33, 49, 62, 74, 77, 86, 161
coaching 30, 86–8, 159
co-creation dilemmas 109
co-evolution 49, 100
cognitive contagion 79
collaboration 11, 13, 26, 30, 45, 62, 76, 107, 123, 135, 157; *see also* E-collaboration
collaborative wisdom 50, 153
collective intelligence-in-action 70, 106; *see also* intelligence–in–action (three levels)
collective learning 69, 103–5, 121; *see also* team learning
commitment 18, 30, 35, 50, 58, 62–3, 69, 74, 76–8, 86, 109–14, 143, 145, 158, 161–2
communal mental maps 70
communities of practice 69–70, 105, 107, 120
community level social capital 77
complex 1–6, 12, 19, 49, 58, 67–70, 72, 74–6, 81, 87–9, 92, 104–6, 113, 124, 140–1, 156; *see also* complicated

INDEX

complex adaptive system 67, 75, 81
complexity 1–10, 28, 44, 49, 68, 73, 76–81, 102–6, 108, 113, 121, 140, 143; *see also* attractors; dissipative structures; fractal
complicated 3–5, 92, 95
conflict issues 62, 86, 94, 141
connectedness 69, 78–9, 105, 159; *see also* 'connectedness' norms
'connectedness' norms 79
consensus 1, 5, 12, 17, 19, 20–9, 43, 54–5, 58, 61–2, 64, 89, 152–4
corporate citizenship behaviour 63, 77
critical reflection 6–7, 34, 41, 53, 87–9, 103, 108, 111, 123, 158
crowdsourcing 10, 37–41, 54, 67, 152, 159
cultural beliefs 102, 159
cultural safety 141
culture 12, 19–20, 40–1, 68, 90, 104, 120, 140–2, 157, 159–61
Cybereconomy 101
Cynefin framework 3–6, 8–10, 19, 30, 34, 44–5, 54, 80, 88, 91, 121

decision making 4–5, 9, 19–22, 25, 45, 55–7, 62, 73, 78, 86, 92, 112–13, 119, 122, 146, 154–5
dialectical 69, 109
dialogue 10, 17, 19–24, 29, 41, 55, 61–4, 69, 85, 87, 88–91, 107, 110, 119, 123, 133, 154, 161
discontinuous change 119
dissipative structures 74, 106; *see also* complexity
double-loop learning 7, 54, 103, 109

E-collaboration 123
edge of chaos 68, 80
embedding 2, 72, 75–6, 115, 141, 159
embedding contexts 72, 141

embodiment 18, 39, 73–6, 111, 115
emcee 85, 154
emergence 1–10, 29–33, 49, 58, 70–2, 75, 88, 123, 161
emergence team stages 54–62, 71–9
emotional regime types 31, 58, 74–5, 79–81, 104, 112–15, 159
enactive team construction 76
epistemology 7, 70, 109
E-web metric 111–13

FAB (features, advantages, benefits) 114
feedback loop 6, 53
focus 4, 9, 13, 26–7, 51–2, 59–61, 72, 76–80, 88–93, 107, 113, 119, 122–3, 131, 134, 140, 154–61
forming stage 13, 54–7, 60; *see also* Tuckman model
fractal 106; *see also* complexity

goal structure 6–7, 53–4, 121
group emotions 73–9
groupthink 24, 62, 73, 77, 145
Guardian 45–6, 58–9

human computer interaction 142–3
human robot interaction 142

idealist 45–6, 58–60
imminent surprise 6, 29, 103–4, 108, 156; *see also* discontinuous change
institutional 72, 90, 159–60
integrative 120
intelligence–in-action (three levels) 107; *see also* collective intelligence
internet of things 156
interviewing 43, 85–7, 95–6, 126–9, 155
intuitive artistry 70, 76, 107–11
irreversible 104
iterative cycles 56–8, 155

knowable environment 19, 58
knowledge production 100, 108
knowledge sharing 10–12, 23–4, 43–7
known environment 19, 58

leadership role 1, 12, 49–54, 73–5, 104, 120–1, 150–3
leadership style 60, 111, 159–60
learning thresholds 103–4
levels of dissent 24; *see also* conflict issues
liminal 101, 103, 143
local rules of engagement 7, 21–6, 76

member temperaments 45–6, 58–60
mental models 43, 69, 88, 95, 102, 106, 109–10, 141–2
metaphor 56, 69–75, 90–1, 105–6, 110–11, 154–5
metonymy 71, 111
micromanage 62
'm' individual 69
mood convergence 79
multi-foci perspective 158
multi-ontological 10, 85
multi-spiral process 75, 105

negotiating styles 141
networks 10–12, 28, 34, 36, 80, 101, 123, 134, 146, 160, 162
Network Visualization Analysis (NVA) 52
norming 13, 54, 57, 61, 155; *see also* Tuckman model

ontology 9–10, 70–1, 85, 109
organization of work 112, 160

paradigmatic 85
patterns 4, 74, 79, 102, 113, 122, 132, 144
performance blockages 13

performance learning 64, 88, 155
performance model (Focus, Will, Capability) 51–2, 122, 154, 157
performing 13, 34–5, 54, 58, 61, 155
personality structure 68, 74, 106
perspective taking 86
phase shift 72–5, 113; *see also* qualitative shift
'p' individual 68–9; *see also* personality structure and 'm' individual
point attractor 79
praxiological (effectiveness) 64
probe (unknowable complex) 58
profiles of commitment 78
project/work commitment 74, 111–12
punctuated equilibria 63

qualitative shift 75; *see also* complexity; edge of chaos; phase shift

Rational 45–6, 58–60, 91, 105–6, 109; *see also* Artisan; Guardian
reflection-in-action 103, 108–9
relative autonomy 75
reliability 100
requisite variety 10
responsible professionals 112–13
rule-boundaries 6, 53

selective perception 79
self-managing teams 88
self-transcendence 71, 75
sense (known and knowable) 58; *see also* Cynefin framework
sensemaking 6, 9–12, 24, 34, 43, 55–7, 79, 88–9, 154–5
serendipitous 'branching out' 70
shared ambivalence 73
silos 144
simple 3–5, 6, 92

single-loop learning 6, 53; *see also* double-loop learning
sociable transformations 70
social identity 68, 74–7, 79, 108
socio-emotional norms 74
splits 112; *see also* emotional regimes; responsible professionals
stable loop attractor 79
stakeholder 17–20, 50, 101, 113, 150, 153, 162
storming 13, 54–5, 57, 61, 154; *see also* Tuckman model
story-based team formation 37–8, 97
storytelling 5, 56, 70, 89–90, 95, 108, 130–1
surface (the 'undiscussables') 110
syntagmatic 69
systemic structure 60, 71, 102
systems thinking, four levels 102

tacit knowledge capture 70, 103, 108–9
task forces 44
team behaviours 6, 12, 39, 45, 53, 62, 73–4, 79, 102–7, 160
team conversations 72, 74–5, 79, 103, 123, 131, 144
team dissent 24–8, 72, 156; *see also* conflict
team dynamics 2, 26–8
team embedding context 75–6, 141
team formation 17; *see also* crowdsourcing; story-based team formation
team identity 62–3, 68, 74–6, 77, 79, 100, 108
team leader as action/performance learning adviser 63–4, 88, 154
team leader's scoreboard 50, 121
team learning 75
team levels of significance 68

team member characteristics 38–42, 45, 54, 73
team personality structure 68; *see also* 'm' individual and 'p' individual
team scaffolding 67
team social capital 12, 77–8
team sponsor 1, 10, 17–20, 23, 28, 29–31, 33–5, 38–9, 41–2, 49–51, 55, 57–8, 85, 151–4, 156–7
team story 57, 68, 75, 97, 103, 106–7, 110, 131, 156, 161
thresholds of change 103–4
tools and techniques 27, 107, 110, 111
transactive memory 74
triple impact evaluation 63
trust 7, 12–13, 24–30, 34–5, 40, 42, 46–7, 58, 61–2, 69, 73, 77–81, 94, 100, 111–13, 141, 145, 158, 161
trusty followers 112–13
Tuckman model 13, 54, 105

unknowable environment 19, 58; *see also* complexity
unlearning 50, 75, 101, 153
un-order 9, 85

Virtual Action Learning (VAL) 125
virtual teaming 141, 143–5
VUCA 1–2, 4–10, 12, 27, 29, 34, 49, 68, 72, 77, 101, 114, 134, 150, 161–2

walkback 110–11
will (to act) 51–2, 72, 78, 80, 91, 94–5, 113, 122, 154, 156–7; *see also* performance model

zones of interaction 160